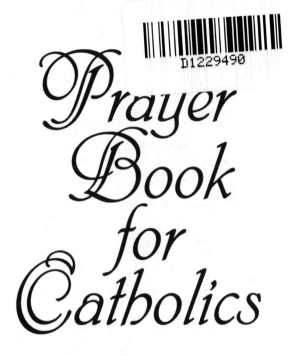

Prayer Book for Catholics

Jacquelyn Lindsey, Editor

Our Sunday Visitor Publishing Division
Our Sunday Visitor, Inc.
Huntington, Indiana 46750

Scripture citations, unless otherwise noted, are from the *Revised Standard Version, Catholic Edition* (RSV), copyright © 1965 and 1966 by the Division of Christian Education of the National Council of Churches of Christ in the U.S.A. and are used by permission of the copyright owner.

Excerpts from the English translation of *Rite of Holy Week* © 1972, International Committee on English in the Liturgy, Inc. (ICEL); excerpts from the English translation of *The Roman Missal* © 1973, ICEL; excerpts from the English translation of *Pastoral Care of the Sick: Rites of Anointing and Viaticum* © 1982, ICEL; excerpts from the English translation of *A Book of Prayers* © 1982, ICEL; excerpts from the English translation of *Order of Christian Funerals* © 1985, ICEL; excerpts from the *Book of Blessings* © 1988, ICEL; English translations of The Apostles' Creed, *Te Deum Laudamus,* and *Nunc Dimittis* by the International Consultation on English Texts (ICET). All rights reserved.

Catechism excerpts are from the English translation of the *Catechism of the Catholic Church, Second Edition,* for use in the United States of America, copyright © 1994 and 1997, United States Catholic Conference - Libreria Editrice Vaticana. Used by permission. All rights reserved.

Every reasonable effort has been made to determine copyright holders and to secure permissions as needed. If any copyrighted materials have been inadvertently used without proper credit being given in one manner or another, please notify Our Sunday Visitor in writing so that future editions may be corrected accordingly.

Table of Contents

Preface

✛

$\mathcal{A}$s spiritual pilgrims, we must focus on the ultimate goal of our journey — to spend eternity in the presence of Our Lord. With that end in mind, prayer should be our constant companion.

If everyone experienced the same events in life, we would only need a few standard prayers. However, life is full of surprises, and no two lives are the same. Today, you may be celebrating a new job, while I might be praying that a friend find employment. One requires a prayer of thanksgiving; the other, a prayer of petition.

The Catholic Church has had two thousand years to develop a significant body of prayers — some exquisite and majestic, others simple and profound. Some may be appropriate only once in a lifetime, while others can be repeated countless times throughout a single day.

There are those who are magnificently articulate in spontaneous prayer. I, on the other hand, find myself lacking in the ability to express myself in prayer that adequately conveys the concerns of my heart. This is why I am so grateful for the traditional prayers of the Church.

I have found prayers for times of sickness and times of health. If I am concerned about family members who are far away, I know I can connect with them through prayer. If I am undecided about what course of action to take, I can pray for guidance.

Some prayers should be committed to memory. The basic prayers in this book should be familiar to all and known by heart. If you don't already know them, pray them daily until they are memorized.

One way to familiarize yourself with the prayers in this book is to pray one new prayer a day. Some, like the

Universal Prayer (pages 80-82), are pages long, but their beauty makes them well worth the time it takes to pray them. Others, like the Aspirations (pages 88-89), are simply one line. Aspirations can be prayed throughout the day, even once an hour.

Integrate prayer into all that you do. Upon awakening, pray for the day ahead of you. Pray for those you love. Pray for your work and your play. Pray for your food and for those who are hungry. Remember prayer during exercise and at rest.

Let prayer be a part of your celebrations. If you have accomplished something new or overcome a challenge, either use a prayer of thanksgiving or simply make a quick Sign of the Cross. If you give someone a gift for birthday or anniversary, pray for him or her as you shop for or wrap the gift.

At times, a prayer partner is a very valuable encouragement for prayer. If you are trying to break a bad habit, knowing someone else is praying for you can be just enough support to help you be successful.

Prayer provides a connection far more effective than phone or e-mail. Distant friends and family are brought closer to heart when we remember them in prayer. They are spiritually with us in a way that distance cannot separate. Even death does not divide us from departed loved ones remembered prayerfully. For those who have gone before us, prayer may be the only gift we can now bestow upon them.

The basic forms of prayer are: blessing, petition, intercession, thanksgiving, and praise. This prayer book contains many examples of each form. Familiarize yourself with the prayers available in all twelve sections, so you will be able to call upon the book's rich treasury of prayers whenever needed.

My prayer for all those who use this book is that the good Lord love you and keep you. May His blessings be yours in abundance always.

— JACQUELYN LINDSEY

I tell you, whatever you ask in prayer, believe
that you will receive it, and you will.

— OUR LORD JESUS CHRIST
(MK. 11:24)

✣

As our body cannot live without nourishment,
so our soul cannot spiritually be kept alive without prayer.

— ST. AUGUSTINE

✣

Virtues are formed by prayer.
Prayer preserves temperance.
Prayer suppresses anger.
Prayer prevents emotions of pride and envy.
Prayer draws into the soul of the Holy Spirit,
    and raises man to heaven.

— ST. EPHRAEM

Basic Prayers

✤

The memorization of basic prayers offers an essential support to the life of prayer, but it is important to help learners savor their meaning.

— *Catechism of the Catholic Church,* NO. 2688

Amen.
(Means: "So be it.")

The Sign of the Cross

In the name of the Father,
And of the Son,
And of the Holy Spirit.
Amen.

We proclaim the Crucified and the devils quake. So don't be ashamed of the cross of Christ. Openly seal it on your forehead that the devils may behold the royal sign and flee trembling far away. Make the Sign of the Cross when you eat or drink, when you sit, lie down or get up, when you speak, when you walk — in a word, at every act.

— St. Cyril of Jerusalem

The Lord's Prayer
(Our Father)

Our Father, who art in heaven,
hallowed be thy name;
thy kingdom come;
thy will be done
on earth as it is in heaven.
Give us this day our daily bread;
and forgive us our trespasses
as we forgive those
who trespass against us;
and lead us not into temptation,
but deliver us from evil.
Amen.

— THE PRAYER JESUS TAUGHT; SEE MT. 6:9-13.

Hail Mary

Hail Mary, full of grace.
The Lord is with thee.
Blessed art thou among women,
and blessed is the fruit of thy womb, Jesus.

Holy Mary, Mother of God,
pray for us sinners,
now and at the hour of our death.
Amen.

— THE ARCHANGEL GABRIEL ANNOUNCES
TO THE VIRGIN MARY THAT SHE WOULD
BEAR THE SON OF GOD, AND ELIZABETH
GREETS MARY; SEE LK. 1:28, 42.

The Glory Be
(The Doxology)

Glory be to the Father,
and to the Son,
and to the Holy Spirit.

As it was in the beginning,
is now, and ever shall be,
world without end.
Amen.

— THIS PRAISE, ACKNOWLEDGING OUR
FAITH IN THE MYSTERY OF THE HOLY TRINITY,
HAS BEEN PRAYED SINCE THE EARLY CHURCH.

Acts of Faith, Hope, and Charity

Act of Faith

O my God, I firmly believe that you are one God in three divine Persons, Father, Son and Holy Spirit; I believe that your divine Son became man and died for our sins, and that he shall come to judge the living and the dead. I believe these and all the truths that the holy Catholic Church teaches, because you have revealed them, who can neither deceive nor be deceived.

Act of Hope

O my God, relying on your almighty power and infinite mercy and promises, I hope to obtain pardon for my sins, the help of your grace, and life everlasting, through the merits of Jesus Christ, my Lord and Redeemer.

Act of Charity (Act of Love)

O my God, I love you above all things, with my whole heart and soul, because you are all good and worthy of all love. I love my neighbor as myself for the love of you. I forgive all who have injured me and ask pardon of all whom I have injured.

— PRAYERS BASED ON THE WORDS OF 1 COR. 13:13:
"SO FAITH, HOPE, LOVE ABIDE, THESE THREE;
BUT THE GREATEST OF THESE IS LOVE."

Apostles' Creed

I believe in God, the Father almighty,
creator of heaven and earth.

I believe in Jesus Christ, his only Son, our Lord.
    He was conceived by the power of the Holy Spirit
        and born of the Virgin Mary.
    He suffered under Pontius Pilate,
        was crucified, died, and was buried.
    He descended to the dead.
    On the third day he rose again.
    He ascended into heaven,
        and is seated at the right hand of the Father.
    He will come again to judge the living and the dead.

I believe in the Holy Spirit,
    the holy catholic Church,
    the communion of saints,
    the forgiveness of sins,
    the resurrection of the body,
    and the life everlasting. Amen.

— THOUGHT TO HAVE ORIGINATED IN THE SECOND CENTURY, THIS PRAYER HAS BEEN USED EVER SINCE TO EXPLAIN THE FAITH THAT THE APOSTLES TAUGHT.

Blessed Trinity

✛

**Prayer is always prayer of the Church; it is
a communion with the Holy Trinity.**
— GENERAL INSTRUCTION,
LITURGY OF THE HOURS 9

May the holy will of God be done in me, for me, and
by me. Glory be to the Father, glory be to the Son, and
glory be to the Holy Spirit. Amen.

Te Deum Laudamus

You are God: we praise you;
You are the Lord: we acclaim you;
You are the eternal Father:
All creation worships you.

To you all angels, all the powers of heaven,
Cherubim and Seraphim, sing in endless praise:
   Holy, holy, holy Lord, God of power and might,
   heaven and earth are full of your glory.

The glorious company of apostles praise you.
The noble fellowship of prophets praise you.
The white-robed army of martyrs praise you.

Throughout the world the holy Church acclaims you:
   Father, of majesty unbounded,
your true and only Son, worthy of all worship,
   and the Holy Spirit, advocate and guide.

You, Christ, are the king of glory,
the eternal Son of the Father.

When you became man to set us free
you did not spurn the Virgin's womb.

You overcame the sting of death,
and opened the kingdom of heaven to all believers.

You are seated at God's right hand in glory.
We believe that you will come, and be our judge.
  Come then, Lord, and help your people,
  bought with the price of your own blood,
  and bring us with your saints
  to glory everlasting.

> — A FOURTH-CENTURY HYMN OF
> PRAISE AND THANKSGIVING

Holy God, We Praise Thy Name

Holy God, we praise thy name!
Lord of all, we bow before thee;
All on earth thy scepter claim,
All in heav'n above adore thee;
Infinite thy vast domain,
Everlasting is thy reign.

Hark! the loud celestial hymn
Angel choirs above are raising;
Cherubim and Seraphim
In unceasing chorus praising,
Fill the heav'ns with sweet accord:
Holy, holy, holy Lord!

Lo! the apostolic train
Join the sacred Name to hallow;

Prophets swell the loud refrain,
And the white-robed martyrs follow;
And from morn to set of sun,
Through the Church the song goes on.

Holy Father, Holy Son,
Holy Spirit, Three we name thee,
While in essence only One,
Undivided God we claim thee,
And adoring bend the knee,
While we own the mystery.

— AN ENGLISH PARAPHRASE OF THE *TE DEUM*

The Divine Praises

Blessed be God.
Blessed be his holy name.
Blessed be Jesus Christ, true God and true man.
Blessed be the name of Jesus.
Blessed be his most sacred heart.
Blessed be his most precious blood.
Blessed be Jesus in the most holy sacrament of the
    altar.
Blessed be the Holy Spirit, the Paraclete.
Blessed be the great mother of God, Mary most
    holy.
Blessed be her holy and immaculate conception.
Blessed be her glorious assumption.
Blessed be the name of Mary, virgin and mother.
Blessed be St. Joseph, her most chaste spouse.
Blessed be God in his angels and in his saints.

Some add this anonymous prayer:
May the Heart of Jesus, in the most Blessed
    Sacrament,

Be praised, adored, and loved, with grateful
    affection
At every moment in the tabernacles of the world.
Even to the end of time.
Amen.

God the Father

Prayer of St. Louis-Marie Grignon de Montfort

Our Father who art in heaven, you completely fill
heaven and earth with the immensity of your being; you
are present everywhere; you are in the saints by your
glory, in the damned by your justice, in the good by
your grace, even in sinners by your patience, tolerating
them. Grant that we may always remember that we
come from you and that we may live as your true children. Grant that we may set our true course according
to your will and never swerve from you. Grant that we
may use our every power, our hearts and souls and
strength to tend toward you, and you alone.

A Prayer to God the Father

God be in my head
    and in my understanding.
God be in my eyes
    and in my looking;
God be in my mouth
    and in my speaking.
God be in my heart
    and in my thinking.
God be at my end
    and my departing.

— Sarum Primer, 152

A Prayer of St. Thomas Aquinas

Grant me grace,
O merciful God,
to desire ardently all that is pleasing to thee,
to examine it prudently,
to acknowledge it truthfully,
and to accomplish it perfectly,
for the praise and glory of thy name.
Amen.

A Prayer from the
Imitation of Christ (Book III, 50)

O Lord God, holy Father,
be you now and forever blessed.
For as you will,
   so it has been done;
and what you do is good.
Let your servant rejoice in you,
not in myself or in any other.
You alone are my true joy.
You are my hope and my crown.
You are my gladness and my honor.
O Lord,
what has your servant
   but what has been received from you
      without deserving it?
Yours are the things that you have given and have
  made.
Amen.

God the Son
Prayer of St. Augustine

Lord Jesus, let me know myself and know you,
And desire nothing, save only you.
Let me hate myself and love you.
Let me do everything for the sake of you.
Let me humble myself and exalt you.
Let me die to myself and live in you.
Let me accept whatever happens as from you.
Let me banish self and follow you.
Let me fly from myself and take refuge in you,
That I may deserve to be defended by you.
Let me fear for myself, let me fear you,
And let me be among those who are chosen by you.
Let me distrust myself and put my trust in you.
Let me be willing to obey for the sake of you.
Let me cling to nothing, save only to you,
And let me be poor because of you.
Call me, that I may see you,
And forever enjoy you.
Amen.

Prayer to the Infant Jesus of Prague

O miraculous Infant Jesus, prostrate before your sacred image, we beseech you to cast a merciful look on our troubled hearts. Let your tender Heart, so inclined to pity, be softened by our prayers, and grant us that grace for which we ardently implore you. Take from us all affliction and despair, all trials and misfortunes with which we are laden. For your sacred infancy's sake, hear our prayers and send us consolation and aid, that we may praise you, with the Father and the Holy Spirit, forever and ever.

Amen.[1]

Prayer to the Sacred Heart of Jesus

Most sacred, most loving Heart of Jesus, you are concealed in the Holy Eucharist, and you beat for us still. Now, as then, you say: "With desire I have desired." I worship you with all my best love and awe, with fervent affection, with my most subdued, most resolved will. For a while you take up your abode within me. O make my heart beat with your Heart! Purify it of all that is earthly, all that is proud and sensual, of all perversity, of all disorder. So fill it with you, that neither the events of the day, nor the circumstances of the time, may have the power to ruffle it; but that in your love and your fear, it may have peace. Amen.[2]

— VEN. JOHN HENRY NEWMAN

Novena of Confidence

Lord Jesus, to Thy Sacred Heart, I confide (mention your request here). Only look! Then do what Your Heart inspires. Let Your Heart decide. I count on it. I trust in it. I throw myself on its mercy. Lord Jesus, You will not fail me!

Amen.[3]

God the Holy Spirit
The *Veni Creator*

Come, Spirit Creator,
    come live in our minds
    and fill our hearts which you have made,
    with perfect grace.

We know you as the Paraclete,
    the gift of God most high,

our fire, our love, the living fountain
and holy anointing of our lives.

With seven gifts you act as
the finger of the Father's right hand;
you are his promised One,
teaching us heavenly speech and
understanding.

Kindle us with fire brought from above,
pour love into our hearts,
and give strength
to our weakness of body.

Drive Satan far away from us,
and give us lasting peace
so that, led by your guidance,
no harm will come to us.

Let us know the Father, through you.
Let us know the Son, through you.
Let us believe forever that you are
the Spirit proceeding from
the Father and the Son.

Glory to the Father,
and glory to his Son,
who rose from death;
and glory to you, kind Strengthener,
forever and ever.
Amen.

Veni, Sancte Spiritus

Holy Spirit, Lord of life,
From your clear celestial height
Your pure beaming radiance give.

Come, O Father of the poor;
Come, with treasure that endure;
Come, O light of all who live.

You of all consolers best,
Visiting the troubled breast,
True refreshing peace bestow.

You in toil our comfort sweet,
Pleasant coolness in the heat,
Solace in the midst of woe.

Light immortal, Light divine,
Visit now these hearts of thine
And our inmost being fill.

If you take your grace away,
Nothing pure in us will stay;
All our good is turned to ill.

Heal our wounds, our strength renew;
On our dryness, pour your dew:
Wash the stains of guilt away.

Bend the stubborn heart and will;
Melt the frozen, warm the chill;
Guide the steps that go astray.

You, on those who evermore
Confess you and still adore,
In your sevenfold gifts descent.

Give them comfort when they die,
Give them life with you on high;
Give them joys that never end.
Amen.

Aspirations to the Holy Spirit
(Prayer of St. Augustine)

Breathe in me, O Holy Spirit,
That my thoughts may all be holy;
Act in me, O Holy Spirit,
That my work, too, may be holy;
Draw my heart, O Holy Spirit,
That I love but what is holy;
Strengthen me, O Holy Spirit,
To defend all that is holy;
Guard me, then, O Holy Spirit,
That I always may be holy.
Amen.

Litanies

A litany is a form of prayer using repetition of phrases and is sometimes chanted. Most are based on Scripture and developed over time. The Litany of the Saints is sometimes used in the Mass (for baptism and ordination).

Litany of the Holy Name

Lord, have mercy.   **Lord, have mercy.**
Christ, have mercy.   **Christ, have mercy.**
Lord, have mercy.   **Lord, have mercy.**
God our Father in heaven . . .   **have mercy on us.**
God the Son, Redeemer of the world . . . **have mercy on us.**
God, the Holy Spirit . . . **have mercy on us.**
Holy Trinity, one God . . . **have mercy on us.**
Jesus, Son of the living God . . . **have mercy on us.**
Jesus, splendor of the Father . . . **have mercy on us.**
Jesus, brightness of everlasting light . . .**have mercy on us.**
Jesus, king of glory . . . **have mercy on us.**
Jesus, dawn of justice . . . **have mercy on us.**
Jesus, Son of the Virgin Mary . . . **have mercy on us.**
Jesus, worthy of our wonder . . . **have mercy on us.**
Jesus, mighty God . . . **have mercy on us.**
Jesus, father of the world to come . . . **have mercy on us.**

Jesus, prince of peace . . . **have mercy on us.**
Jesus, all-powerful . . . **have mercy on us.**
Jesus, pattern of patience . . . **have mercy on us.**
Jesus, model of obedience . . . **have mercy on us.**
Jesus, gentle and humble of heart . . . **have mercy on us.**
Jesus, lover of chastity . . . **have mercy on us.**
Jesus, lover of us all . . . **have mercy on us.**
Jesus, God of peace . . . **have mercy on us.**
Jesus, author of life . . . **have mercy on us.**
Jesus, model of goodness . . . **have mercy on us.**
Jesus, seeker of souls . . . **have mercy on us.**
Jesus, our God . . . **have mercy on us.**
Jesus, our refuge . . . **have mercy on us.**
Jesus, father of the poor . . . **have mercy on us.**
Jesus, treasure of the faithful . . . **have mercy on us.**
Jesus, Good Shepherd . . . **have mercy on us.**
Jesus, the true light . . . **have mercy on us.**
Jesus, eternal wisdom . . . **have mercy on us.**
Jesus, infinite goodness . . . **have mercy on us.**
Jesus, our way and our life . . . **have mercy on us.**
Jesus, joy of angels . . . **have mercy on us.**
Jesus, king of patriarchs . . . **have mercy on us.**
Jesus, teacher of apostles . . . **have mercy on us.**
Jesus, master of evangelists . . **have mercy on us.**
Jesus, courage of martyrs . . . **have mercy on us.**
Jesus, light of confessors . . . **have mercy on us.**
Jesus, purity of virgins . . . **have mercy on us.**
Jesus, crown of all saints . . . **have mercy on us.**
Lord, be merciful . . . **Jesus, save your people.**
From all evil . . . **Jesus, save your people.**
From every sin . . . **Jesus, save your people.**
From the snares of the devil . . . **Jesus, save your people.**
From your anger . . . **Jesus, save your people.**

From the spirit of infidelity . . . **Jesus, save your people.**

From everlasting death . . . **Jesus, save your people.**

From neglect of your Holy Spirit . . . **Jesus, save your people.**

By the mystery of your incarnation . . . **Jesus, save your people.**

By your birth . . . **Jesus, save your people.**

By your childhood . . . **Jesus, save your people.**

By your hidden life . . . **Jesus, save your people.**

By your public ministry . . . **Jesus, save your people.**

By your agony and crucifixion . . . **Jesus, save your people.**

By your abandonment . . . **Jesus, save your people.**

By your grief and sorrow . . . **Jesus, save your people.**

By your death and burial . . . **Jesus, save your people.**

By your rising to new life . . . **Jesus, save your people.**

By your return in glory to the Father . . . **Jesus, save your people.**

By your gift of the Holy Spirit . . . **Jesus, save your people.**

By your gift of the Holy Eucharist . . . **Jesus, save your people.**

By your joy and glory . . . **Jesus, save your people.**

Christ, hear us.	**Christ, hear us.**
Lord Jesus, hear our prayer.	**Lord Jesus, hear our prayer.**
Lamb of God, you take away the sins of the world,	**Have mercy on us.**
Lamb of God, you take away the sins of the world,	**Have mercy on us.**
Lamb of God, you take away the sins of the world,	**Have mercy on us.**

Let us pray:

Lord, may we who honor the holy name of Jesus
   enjoy his friendship in this life and be filled with
   eternal joy in the kingdom where he lives and
   reigns forever and ever.
R. Amen.[4]

Litany of the Blessed Virgin Mary
(Also called the Litany of Loreto)

Lord, have mercy on us.	**Christ, have mercy on us.**
Lord, have mercy on us.	
Christ, hear us.	**Christ, graciously hear us.**
God the Father of heaven,	**Have mercy on us.**
God the Son, Redeemer of the world,	**Have mercy on us.**
God the Holy Spirit,	**Have mercy on us.**
Holy Trinity, one God,	**Have mercy on us.**
Holy Mary . . .	**pray for us.**
Holy Mother of God . . .	**pray for us.**
Holy Virgin of virgins . . .	**pray for us.**
Mother of Christ . . .	**pray for us.**
Mother of the Church . . .	**pray for us.**
Mother of divine grace . . .	**pray for us.**
Mother most pure . . .	**pray for us.**
Mother most chaste . . .	**pray for us.**
Mother inviolate . . .	**pray for us.**
Mother undefiled . . .	**pray for us.**
Mother immaculate . . .	**pray for us.**
Mother most amiable . . .	**pray for us.**
Mother most admirable	**pray for us.**
Mother of good counsel . . .	**pray for us.**
Mother of our Creator . . .	**pray for us.**
Mother of our Savior . . .	**pray for us.**

Virgin most prudent . . .	**pray for us.**
Virgin most venerable . . .	**pray for us.**
Virgin most renowned . . .	**pray for us.**
Virgin most powerful . . .	**pray for us.**
Virgin most merciful . . .	**pray for us.**
Virgin most faithful . . .	**pray for us.**
Mirror of justice . . .	**pray for us.**
Seat of wisdom . . .	**pray for us.**
Cause of our joy . . .	**pray for us.**
Spiritual vessel . . .	**pray for us.**
Vessel of honor . . .	**pray for us.**
Singular vessel of devotion . . .	**pray for us.**
Mystical rose . . .	**pray for us.**
Tower of David . . .	**pray for us.**
Tower of ivory . . .	**pray for us.**
House of gold . . .	**pray for us.**
Ark of the covenant . . .	**pray for us.**
Gate of heaven . . .	**pray for us.**
Morning star . . .	**pray for us.**
Health of the sick . . .	**pray for us.**
Refuge of sinners . . .	**pray for us.**
Comforter of the afflicted . . .	**pray for us.**
Help of Christians . . .	**pray for us.**
Queen of angels . . .	**pray for us.**
Queen of patriarchs . . .	**pray for us.**
Queen of prophets . . .	**pray for us.**
Queen of apostles . . .	**pray for us.**
Queen of martyrs . . .	**pray for us.**
Queen of confessors . . .	**pray for us.**
Queen of virgins . . .	**pray for us.**
Queen of all saints . . .	**pray for us.**
Queen conceived without original sin . . .	**pray for us.**
Queen assumed into heaven . . .	**pray for us.**
Queen of the most holy Rosary . . .	**pray for us.**
Queen of peace . . .	**pray for us.**

V. Lamb of God, You take away the sins of the world,
R. Spare us, O Lord.
V. Lamb of God, You take away the sins of the world,
R. Graciously hear us, O Lord.
V. Lamb of God, You take away the sins of the world,
R. Have mercy on us.

V. Pray for us, O holy Mother of God.
R. That we may be made worthy of the promises of Christ.

Let us pray.
O God, whose only-begotten Son, by his life, death, and resurrection, has purchased for us the rewards of everlasting life; grant, we beseech you, that we who meditate on these mysteries of the most holy Rosary of the Blessed Virgin Mary, may both imitate what they contain, and obtain what they promise. Through the same, Christ our Lord. Amen.

A pious custom suggests adding the following prayers after the litany:

For the needs of the Church and of the nation:
Our Father, Hail Mary, Glory Be.

For the (arch)bishop of this diocese and his intentions:
Our Father, Hail Mary, Glory Be.

For the holy souls in purgatory:
Our Father, Hail Mary, May they rest in peace.
R. Amen.

Litany of the Saints

When a person is in danger of death, the litany may be prayed for him or her with special mention of the person's patron saint. This litany is also prayed at Easter, baptisms, and ordinations.

Lord, have mercy.	**Lord, have mercy.**
Christ, have mercy.	**Christ, have mercy.**
Lord, have mercy.	**Lord, have mercy.**
Holy Mary, Mother of God . . .	**pray for us (him/her).**
Holy angels of God . . .	**pray for us (him/her).**
St. John the Baptist . . .	**pray for us (him/her).**
St. Joseph . . .	**pray for us (him/her).**
St. Peter and St. Paul . . .	**pray for us (him/her).**
St. Andrew . . .	**pray for us (him/her).**
St. John . . .	**pray for us (him/her).**
St. Mary Magdalene . . .	**pray for us (him/her).**
St. Stephen . . .	**pray for us (him/her).**
St. Ignatius . . .	**pray for us (him/her).**
St. Lawrence . . .	**pray for us (him/her).**
St. Perpetua and St. Felicity . . .	**pray for us (him/her).**
St. Agnes . . .	**pray for us (him/her).**
St. Gregory . . .	**pray for us (him/her).**
St. Augustine . . .	**pray for us (him/her).**
St. Athanasius . . .	**pray for us (him/her).**
St. Basil . . .	**pray for us (him/her).**
St. Martin . . .	**pray for us (him/her).**
St. Benedict . . .	**pray for us (him/her).**
St. Francis and St. Dominic . . .	**pray for us (him/her).**
St. Francis Xavier . . .	**pray for us (him/her).**
St. John Vianney . . .	**pray for us (him/her).**
St. Catherine . . .	**pray for us (him/her).**

St. Teresa . . . **pray for us (him/her).**
(other saints may be included here)
All holy men and women . . . **pray for us (him/her).**
Lord, be merciful . . . **Lord, save your people.**
From all evil . . . **Lord, save your people.**
From every sin . . . **Lord, save your people.**
From Satan's power . . . **Lord, save your people.**
At the moment of death . . . **Lord, save your people.**
From everlasting death . . . **Lord, save your people.**
On the day of judgment . . . **Lord, save your people.**
By your coming as man . . . **Lord, save your people.**
By your suffering and cross . . . **Lord, save your people.**
By your death and rising to new life . . . **Lord, save your people.**
By your return in glory to the Father . . . **Lord, save your people.**
By your gift of the Holy Spirit . . . **Lord, save your people.**
By your coming again in glory . . . **Lord, save your people.**
Be merciful to us sinners; **Lord, hear our prayer.**
Bring N. to eternal life, first promised to him (her) in Baptism . . . **Lord, hear our prayer.**
Raise N. on the last day, for he (she) has eaten the Bread of life . . . **Lord, hear our prayer.**
Let N. share in your glory, for he (she) has shared in your suffering and death . . . **Lord, hear our prayer.**
Jesus, Son of the living God . . . **Lord, hear our prayer.**
Christ, hear us. **Christ, hear us.**
Lord Jesus, hear our prayer. **Lord Jesus, hear our prayer.**[5]

Mary

✠

The prayer of the Church is sustained by the prayer of Mary and united with it in hope.
— *Catechism of the Catholic Church,*
NO. 2679

Hail Mary
(See page 9)

The *Magnificat*
(See page 91-92)

Sub Tuum Presidium

We fly to your patronage,
    O holy Mother of God;
despise not our petitions in our necessities,
    but deliver us from all danger,
O glorious and blessed Virgin.
Amen.

The *Memorare*

Remember, O most gracious Virgin Mary, that never was it known that anyone who fled to your protection, implored your help, or sought your intercession was left unaided.

Inspired by this confidence I fly unto you, O virgin of virgins, my Mother. To you do I come, before you I stand, sinful and sorrowful. O Mother of the Word Incarnate, despise not my petitions, but in your mercy, hear and answer me. Amen.

Hail, Holy Queen
(Salve Regina)

Hail, holy Queen, Mother of Mercy. Hail, our life, our sweetness and our hope. To you do we cry, poor banished children of Eve. To you do we send up our sighs, mourning and weeping in this valley of tears. Turn, then, most gracious advocate, your eyes of mercy toward us and after this, our exile, show unto us the blessed fruit of your womb, Jesus. O clement, O loving, O sweet Virgin Mary.

Queen of Heaven
(Regina Coeli)

O Queen of Heaven, rejoice, alleluia.
For he whom you were privileged to bear, alleluia,
Has risen as he said, alleluia.
Pray for us to God, alleluia.
Rejoice and be glad, O Virgin Mary, alleluia.
For the Lord has truly risen, alleluia.

Let us pray: O God, you gave joy to the world through the Resurrection of your Son, our Lord Jesus Christ, grant that we may obtain, through his Virgin Mother, Mary, the joys of everlasting life. Through the same Christ our Lord. Amen.

Hail, Queen of the Heavens
(Ave Regina Coelorum)

Hail, Queen of the heavens!
Hail, Empress of the angels!
Hail, Root of Jesse, gate of morn!
From you the world's true Light was born.

Rejoice, glorious Virgin
Lovelier than all the other virgins in heaven.
You are fairer than all the fair,
Plead with Christ, our sins to spare.
Amen.

The *Stabat Mater*

At the Cross her station keeping
Stood the mournful Mother weeping,
   Close to Jesus to the last.

Through her heart his sorrow sharing,
All his bitter anguish bearing,
   Lo! the piercing sword had passed.

For his people's sins rejected,
Saw her Jesus unprotected,
   Saw with thorns, with scourges rent.

Saw her Son from judgment taken,
Her beloved in death forsaken,
   Till his spirit forth he sent.

Jesus, may your Cross defend me,
And your Mother's prayer befriend me.
   Let me die in your embrace.

When to dust my dust returns
Grant a soul, which for you yearns,
   In your Paradise a place. Amen.

Prayer to Our Lady, Help of Christians

O heavenly Lady, help of Christians, I come to you, for you never refuse help to anyone. Mary, help of Christians, you have often answered the prayers of nations. You have helped the Pope, bishops, priests, religious, all Christians. Whenever those who love you put their hope in you, you hurry to them with a mother's love. Your greatest wish is to help the holy Church of your Son still here on earth.

My mother, my hope, O Lady, help of Christians, make me live in the love of your holy Son, Jesus Christ. Help me in my every need.[6]

Prayer to Our Lady for Protection

O holy Virgin, Mother of God, my Mother and Patroness, I place myself under thy protection; I throw myself with confidence into the arms of thy compassion. Be to me, O Mother of mercy, my refuge in distress, my consolation under suffering, my advocate with thy adorable Son, now and at the hour of my death. Amen.[7]

Miraculous Medal Prayer

O Mary conceived without sin,
pray for us who have recourse to you.

Prayer to Our Lady of Guadalupe

Our Lady of Guadalupe, mystical Rose, make intercession for our Holy Church, protect the Pope, help all those who invoke you in their necessities, and since you are the ever Virgin Mary and Mother of the true God, obtain for us from your most Holy Son, the grace of keeping our faith, sweet hope in the midst of the bitterness of life, burning charity, and the precious gift of final perseverance. Amen.

Loving Mother of the Redeemer
(Alma Redemptoris Mater)

O loving Mother of the Redeemer,
Gate of Heaven, Star of the Sea,
Assist your people who have fallen,
   yet strive to rise again.

To the wonder of nature, you bore your Creator,
Yet remained a Virgin, after as before,
You who received Gabriel's joyful greeting,
   have pity on us poor sinners. Amen.

Our Lady of Lourdes

Our Lady of Lourdes, please come to the assistance of all those who are suffering. Amen.

Help Us, Mother

O Jesus, you paid our debts by your death.
O dear Mother, you gave him to us so we could be
   saved.
God did not choose great people for his messengers
   and his channels of love.
Only the humble can see clearly.
And only they say we are nothing, and God is
   everything.
How blessed you are, dear Jesus, and how loving is
   your Mother.
Please help us and bless us. Amen. *(cont.)*

The world proclaims the gospel of money;
Jesus proclaims the gospel of love.
Help us, Mother, to love your Son more
and follow his holy Gospel. Amen.[8]

Unfailing Help

Let us move forward in the joy of the Risen Lord,
confident of his unfailing help! The Lord will
help us, and Mary, his Most Holy Mother, will
be on our side.

— POPE BENEDICT XVI

Novena to Mary, Queen of all Hearts

O Mary, Queen of All Hearts, advocate of the most
hopeless cases; Mother most pure, most
compassionate; Mother of Divine Love, full of
divine light, we confide to your care the favors
which we ask of you today.

Consider our misery, our tears, our interior trials and
sufferings! We know that you can help us through
the merits of your Divine Son, Jesus. We promise,
if our prayers are heard, to spread your glory, by
making you known under the title of Mary, Queen
of All Hearts, Queen of the Universe.

Grant, we beseech you, hear our prayers, for every day
you give us so many proofs of your love and your
power of intercession to heal both body and soul.

We hope against hope: Ask Jesus to cure us, pardon
us, and grant us final perseverance.

O Mary, Queen of All Hearts, help us, we have
confidence in you (*three times*).

The Rosary

The Rosary should be prayed year round, but special effort should be made during October, the month of the Rosary.

On the crucifix, pray: the Apostles' Creed
On the first large bead, pray: one Our Father
On the next three small beads, pray: three Hail Marys
Pray: one Glory Be

Each decade of the rosary consists of one Our Father (on the large beads), ten Hail Marys (on the small beads) and one Glory Be. Many then add the Fatima invocation: "O my Jesus, forgive us our sins, save us from the fires of hell and lead all souls to heaven, especially those most in need of thy mercy."

The Joyful Mysteries

(SAID ON MONDAYS AND SATURDAYS)

1. The Annunciation of the birth of the Lord to Mary by the archangel Gabriel (Lk. 1:26-38).
2. The Visitation of Our Lady with St. Elizabeth, the mother of St. John the Baptist (Lk. 1:39-56).
3. The Nativity of Our Lord (Mt. 1:18-25; Lk. 2:1-20).
4. The Presentation of the Christ Child in the Temple (Lk. 2:22-32).
5. The Finding of the Child Jesus in the Temple (Lk. 2:41-52).

The Luminous Mysteries

(SAID ON THURSDAYS)

1. The Baptism of Jesus (Mt. 3:16).
2. The Wedding Feast of Cana (Jn. 2:4-5, 11).
3. The Invitation of Jesus (Mk. 1:14-15).
4. The Transfiguration (Lk. 9:29-35).
5. The Eucharist (Mt. 26:26-27).

The Sorrowful Mysteries

(SAID ON TUESDAYS AND FRIDAYS)

1. The Agony in the Garden of Gethsemane (Mk. 14:32-42).
2. The Scourging at the Pillar (Jn. 19:1).
3. The Crowning with Thorns (Mk. 15:16-20).
4. The Carrying of the Cross (Jn. 19:12-16).
5. The Crucifixion (Mt. 27:33-56; Mk. 15:22-41; Lk. 23:26-49; Jn. 19:16-30)

The Glorious Mysteries

(SAID ON WEDNESDAYS AND SUNDAYS)

1. The Resurrection (Lk. 24:1-12; Jn. 20).
2. The Ascension (Lk 24:50-53; Acts 1:1-12).
3. The Descent of the Holy Spirit at Pentecost (Acts 2:1-4).
4. The Assumption of the Blessed Virgin Mary (Song 2:8-14).
5. The Coronation of the Blessed Mother (Rev 12:1-4).

Concluding Prayer:

Hail, holy Queen, Mother of Mercy. Hail, our life, our sweetness and our hope. To you do we cry, poor banished children of Eve. To you do we send up our sighs, mourning, and weeping in this valley of tears. Turn, then, most gracious advocate, your eyes of mercy toward us and after this, our exile, show unto us the blessed fruit of your womb, Jesus. O clement, O loving, O sweet Virgin Mary.

V. Pray for us, O Holy Mother of God.

R. That we made be made worthy of the promises of Christ.
Let us pray:

O God, whose only begotten Son, by his Life, Death and Resurrection has purchased for us the rewards of eternal life, grant, we beseech you, that we who meditate on these mysteries of the most holy Rosary of the Blessed Virgin Mary, may both imitate what they contain and obtain what they promise, by the same Christ Our Lord. Amen.

Saints and Holy Ones

✛

Do not weep; for I shall be more useful to you after my death and I shall help you then more effectively than during my life.

— ST. DOMINIC

St. Alphonsus Liguori
Prayer for Five Graces

Eternal Father, your Son has promised that you would grant all the graces we ask of you in His name. Trusting in this promise, and in the name and through the merits of Jesus Christ, I ask of you five graces:

First, I ask pardon for all offenses I have committed, for which I am sorry with all my heart, because I have offended your infinite goodness.

Second, I ask for your divine Light, which will enable me to see the vanity of all the things of this earth, and see also your infinite greatness and goodness.

Third, I ask for a share in your love, so that I can detach myself from all creatures, especially from myself, and love only your holy will.

Fourth, grant me the grace to have confidence in the merits of Jesus Christ and in the intercession of Mary.

Fifth, I ask for the grace of perseverance, knowing that whenever I call on you for assistance, you will answer my call and come to my aid; I fear only that I will neglect to turn to you in time of need, and thus bring myself to ruin. Grant me the grace to pray always, O Eternal Father, in the name of Jesus.

Amen.[9]

(Attributed to St. Alphonsus Liguori, 1696-1787, Italian bishop and founder of the Redemptorists, who was proclaimed a doctor of the Church and is patron of confessors and moralists. Feast: August 1.)

Bl. André Bessette

Bl. Brother André, your devotion to St. Joseph is an inspiration to us. You gave your life selflessly to bring the message of his life to others. Pray that we may learn from St. Joseph, and from you, what it is like to care for Jesus and do his work in the world. Amen.[10]

(Bl. André Bessette, 1845-1937, was a Canadian Holy Cross brother instrumental in building St. Joseph's Oratory in Montreal, Canada. Feast: January 6.)

St. Anselm of Canterbury
Searching for God

O Lord, my God, teach my heart this day where and how to see you, where and how to find you. You have made me and remade me, and you have bestowed on me all the good things I possess, and still I do not know you. I have not yet done that for which I was made. Teach me to seek you, for I cannot seek you unless you teach me, or find you unless you show yourself to me. Let me seek you in my desire; let me desire you in my seeking. Let me find you by loving you; let me love you when I find you.[11]

(Attributed to St. Anselm, 1033-1109, Italian Benedictine and archbishop of Canterbury, who was proclaimed a doctor of the Church and is called the Father of Scholasticism. Feast: April 21.)

St. Anthony of Padua
Prayer to Recover Lost Things

O blessed St. Anthony, the grace of God has made you a powerful advocate in all our needs and the patron for the restoring of things lost or stolen. I turn to you today with childlike love and deep confidence. You are the counselor of the erring, the comforter of the troubled, the healer of the sick, the refuge of the fallen. You have helped countless children of God to find the things they have lost — material things and, more importantly, the things of the spirit: faith and hope and love. I come to you with confidence. Help me in my present need. I recommend what I have lost to your care, in the hope that God will restore it to me if it is His holy will. Amen.

St. Anthony of Padua Novena

St. Anthony, glorious for the fame of your miracles, obtain for me from God's mercy this favor that I desire: (mention your request here). Since you were so gracious to poor sinners, do not regard my lack of virtue but consider the glory of God, which will be exalted once more through you by the granting of the petition that I now earnestly present to you.

Glorious Wonderworker St. Anthony, father of the poor and comforter of the afflicted, I ask for your help. You have come to my aid with such loving care and have comforted me so generously. I offer you my heartfelt thanks. Accept this offering of my devotion and love and with it my earnest promise, which I now renew, to live always in the love of God and my neighbor. Continue to shield me graciously with your protection, and obtain for me the grace of being able one day to enter the Kingdom of Heaven, there to praise with you the everlasting mercies of God. Amen.

(St. Anthony of Padua, d. 1231, a Franciscan called the "Wonder Worker," was proclaimed a doctor of the Church; patron for finding lost items. Feast: June 13.)

St. Augustine

My God, let me know and love you, so that I may find my happiness in you. Enable me to know you ever more on earth, so that I may know you perfectly in heaven. In that way my joy may be great on earth, and perfect in heaven.

O God of truth, grant me the happiness of heaven so that my joy may be full in accord with your promise. In the meantime let me mind dwell on that happiness, my tongue speak of it, my heart pine for it, my mouth pronounce it, my soul hunger for it, my flesh thirst for it, and my entire being desire it until I enter through death in the joy of my Lord forever. Amen.[12]

(St. Augustine, 354-430, was bishop of Hippo in North Africa; his writings in philosophy and theology made lasting contributions to the Church. Feast: August 28.)

St. Basil the Great
The Ship of Life

Steer the ship of my life, Lord, to your quiet harbor, where I can be safe from the storms of sin and conflict. Show me the course I should take. Renew in me the gift of discernment, so that I can see the right direction in which I should go. And give me the strength and the courage to choose the right course, even when the sea is rough and the waves are high, knowing that through enduring hardship and danger in your name we shall find comfort and peace. Amen.

(St. Basil the Great, c. 330-379, bishop of Caesarea, was proclaimed Father and Doctor of the Church and is called the Father of Monasticism in the East. Feast: January 2.)

St. Benedict of Nursia
For Seekers of Faith

(INSPIRED BY ST. BENEDICT)

Gracious and holy Father, give us the wisdom to discover you, the intelligence to understand you, the diligence to seek after you, the patience to wait for you, eyes to behold you, a heart to meditate on you, and a life to proclaim you, through the power of the spirit of Jesus, our Lord. Amen.

(St. Benedict of Nursia, c. 480-547, an abbot, called the great Father of Western Monasticism, gave the monks his Holy Rule, still in use today; he is patron of Europe. Feast: July 11.)

St. Bernard of Clairvaux
The Sweetness of Divine Love

Jesus, how sweet is the very thought of you! You fill my heart with joy. The sweetness of your love surpasses the sweetness of honey. Nothing sweeter than you can be described; no words can express the joy of your love. Only those who have tasted your love for themselves can comprehend it. In your love you listen to all my prayers, even when my wishes are childish, my words confused, and my thoughts foolish. And you answer my prayers, not according to my own misdirected desires, which would bring only bitter misery; but according to my real needs, which brings me sweet joy. Thank you, Jesus, for giving yourself to me. Amen.

(St. Bernard of Clairvaux, 1090-1153, French monastic reformer, a mystical theologian, helped the spread of Cistercian monks throughout Europe, is called the Mellifluous Doctor. Feast: August 20.)

St. Catherine of Siena

O tender Father,
you gave me more, much more
than I ever thought to ask for.

I realize that our human desires
can never really match
what you long to give us.

Thanks,
and again thanks, O Father,
for having granted my petitions, and
that which I never realized I needed
or petitioned. Amen.

(St. Catherine of Siena, 1347-1380, was an Italian in the Third Order of St. Dominic; a mystic and spiritual writer, she is the second woman named Doctor of the Church. Feast: April 29.)

St. Cecilia

Dear St. Cecilia, one thing we know for certain about you is that you became a heroic martyr in fidelity to your divine Bridegroom.

We do not know that you were a musician, but we are told that you heard angels sing.

Inspire musicians to gladden the hearts of people by filling the air with God's gift of music and reminding them of the divine Musician who created all beauty.

(St. Cecilia, second-third centuries, a Roman virgin and martyr, is the patroness of music. Feast: November 22.)

St. Christopher

Dear Saint, you have inherited a beautiful name — "Christ bearer" — as a result of a wonderful legend that, while carrying people across a raging stream, you also miraculously carried the Child Jesus. Teach us to be true "Christ bearers" to those who do not know Him. Protect all drivers who often transport those who bear Christ within them. Amen.

(St. Christopher, born in Asia Minor, died c. 251; martyred for his faith, he is patron of travelers, archers, and protection against storms. Memorial: July 25.)

St. Clement of Rome
Prayer for Divine Assistance

We beg you, Lord, to help and to defend us. Deliver the oppressed, pity the insignificant, raise the fallen, show yourself to the needy, heal the sick, bring back those of your people who have gone astray, feed the hungry, lift up the weak, take off the prisoners' chains. May every nation come to know that you alone are God, that Jesus Christ is your Child, that we are your people, the sheep that you pasture.[13]

(Inspired by St. Clement of Rome, Pope 88-97; a martyr, he is invoked against disasters at sea, storms, and lightning. Feast: November 23.)

St. Clement of Alexandria
To the Divine Tutor

Be kind to your little children, Lord. Be a gentle teacher, patient with our weakness and stupidity. And give us the strength and discernment to do what you tell us, and so grow in your likeness. May we all live in the peace that comes from you. May we journey toward your city, sailing through the waters of sin untouched by the waves, borne serenely along by the Holy Spirit. Night and day may we give you praise and thanks, because you have shown us that all things belong to you, and all blessings are gifts from you. To you, the essence of wisdom, the foundation of truth, be glory forevermore.

(Inspired by St. Clement of Alexandria, c. 150-215, confessor, teacher, and author of many writings. Feast: December 4.)

St. Cyprian of Carthage
For All Needs

We pray to you, Lord, with honest hearts, in tune with one another, entreating you with sighs and tears, as befits our humble position — placed, as we are, between the spiritually weak who have no concern for you and the saints who stand firm and upright before you. We pray that you may soon come to us, leading us from darkness to light, oppression to freedom, misery to joy, conflict to peace. May you drive away the storms and tempests of our lives, and bring gentle calm. We pray that you will care for us, as a father cares for his children. Amen.

(Inspired by St. Cyprian of Carthage, c. 200-258, who was born in Africa, became bishop of Carthage, and left us many ecclesiastical writings. Feast: September 16.)

St. Dymphna

Lord, our God, you graciously chose St. Dymphna as patroness of those afflicted with mental and nervous disorders. She is thus an inspiration and a symbol of charity to the thousands who ask her intercession.

Please grant, Lord, through the prayers of this pure youthful martyr, relief and consolation to all suffering such trials, especially those for whom we pray. (Here mention those for whom you wish to pray.)

We beg you, Lord, to hear the prayers of St. Dymphna on our behalf. Grant all those for whom we pray patience in their sufferings and resignation to your divine will. Please fill them with hope, and grant them the relief and cure they so much desire.

We ask this though Christ our Lord who suffered agony in the garden. Amen.

(St. Dymphna is the patroness of those afflicted with nervous and mental disorders, emotional distress, or depression. Feast: May 15.)

St. Edmund

Into your hands, O Lord,
and into the hands of your holy angels,
I commit and entrust this day my soul,
    my relations, my benefactors,
    my friends and my enemies,
        and all your people.
Keep us, O Lord, through this day
by the merits and intercession
    of the Blessed Virgin Mary
    and all the saints,
from all vicious and unruly desires,
from all sins and temptations of the devil,
and from sudden and improvided death
and the pains of hell.
Illuminate my heart
    with the grace of your Holy Spirit;
grant that I may ever be obedient
    to your commandments;
suffer me not to be separated from you,
O Lord Jesus Christ,
who lives and reigns
    with God the Father
    and the same Holy Spirit
forever and ever. Amen.

(Inspired by St. Edmund of Abingdon, c. 1175-1240, who was archbishop of Canterbury, England. Feast: November 20.)

St. Elizabeth Ann Seton

Lord God, you blessed Elizabeth Seton with gifts of grace as wife and mother, educator and foundress, so that she might spend her life in service to your people. Through her example and prayers, may we learn to express our love for you in love for our fellow men and women. We ask this through your Son, Jesus Christ, who lives and reigns with you and the Holy Spirit, one God, forever and ever. Amen.

(St. Elizabeth Ann Bayley Seton, 1774-1821, first American-born saint, founded the Sisters of Charity. Feast: January 4.)

St. Faustina Kowalska
Divine Mercy Chaplet

Recite one Our Father, one Hail Mary, and the Apostles" Creed. Then, on the Our Father beads of the rosary, say the following words:

Eternal Father, I offer You the Body and Blood, Soul and Divinity of Your dearly beloved Son, Our Lord Jesus Christ, in atonement for our sins and those of the whole world.

On the Hail Mary beads, say the following words:
For the sake of His sorrowful Passion, have mercy on us and on the whole world.

At the conclusion of each decade, recite three times:
Holy God, Holy Mighty One, Holy Immortal One, have mercy on us and on the whole world.

A Prayer for Divine Mercy

O Greatly Merciful God, Infinite Goodness, today all mankind calls out from the abyss of its misery to Your mercy—to Your compassion, O God; and it is with its mighty voice of misery that it cries out: Gracious God, do not reject the prayer of this earth's exiles! O Lord, Goodness beyond our understanding, Who are acquainted with our misery through and through, and know that by our power we cannot ascend to You, we implore You, anticipate us with Your grace and keep on increasing Your mercy in us, that we may faithfully do Your holy will all through our life and at death's hour. Let the omnipotence of Your mercy shield us from the darts of our salvation's enemies, that we may with confidence, as Your children, await Your final coming — that day known to You alone. And we expect to obtain everything promised us by Jesus in spite of all our wretchedness. For Jesus is our Hope: Through His merciful Heart as through an open gate we pass through to heaven.[14]

— FROM THE DIARY OF ST. FAUSTINA OF
THE SISTERS OF OUR LADY OF MERCY

(St. Faustina Kowalska, 1905-1938, was a humble Polish nun who received the message of Divine Mercy in revelations. The Church celebrates Divine Mercy Sunday on the Sunday after Easter, and the chaplet is prayed beginning on the Easter Vigil. It may also be prayed at other times.)

St. Frances Xavier Cabrini

"Fortify me with the grace of your Holy Spirit and give your peace to my soul that I may be free from all needless anxiety, solicitude and worry. Help me to desire always that which is pleasing and acceptable to you so that your Will may be my will. Grant that I may rid myself of all unholy desires and that, for your love, I may remain obscure and unknown in this world, to be known only to you. Do not permit me to attribute to myself the good that you perform in me and through me, but rather, referring all honor to your Majesty, may I glory only in my infirmities, so that renouncing sincerely all vainglory which comes from the world, I may aspire to that true and lasting glory which comes from you. Amen."

God, our Father, you called Frances Xavier Cabrini from Italy to serve the immigrants of America. By her example, teach us concern for the stranger, the sick, and the frustrated. By her prayers, help us to see Christ in all the men and women we meet. Grant this through our Lord Jesus Christ, your Son, who lives and reigns with you and the Holy Spirit, one God, forever and ever. Amen.

(St. Frances Xavier Cabrini, 1850-1917, an Italian nun, founded the Missionary Sisters of the Sacred Heart, became a citizen, and was the first American citizen to be canonized. Feast: November 13.)

St. Francis of Assisi
Prayer attributed to St. Francis of Assisi

Lord make me an instrument of Your peace:
Where there is hatred, let me sow love.
Where there is injury, pardon,
Where there is doubt, faith,
Where there is despair, hope,

Where there is darkness, light,
and where there is sadness, joy.

O Divine Master, grant that I may not so much
seek to be consoled, as to console;
To be understood, as to understand;
To be loved, as to love;
For it is in giving that we receive,
It is in pardoning that we are pardoned
And it is in dying that we are born to eternal life.

(St. Francis, 1181/82-1226, founded the Franciscan Order, received the sacred stigmata, and is the patron of Italy, Catholic Action, and ecologists. Feast: October 4.)

St. Francis de Sales
Your Cross

The everlasting God has in His wisdom foreseen from eternity the cross that He now presents to you as a gift from His inmost Heart.

This cross He now sends you He has considered with His all-knowing eyes, understood with His Divine mind, tested with His wise justice, warmed with loving arms and weighed with His own hands to see that it be not one inch too large and not one ounce too heavy for you.

He has blessed it with His holy Name, anointed it with His grace, perfumed it with His consolation, taken one last glance at you and your courage, and then sent it to you from heaven, a special greeting from God to you, a gift of the all-merciful love of God. Amen.

(St. Francis de Sales, 1567-1622, bishop of Geneva and devotional writer, was proclaimed a doctor of the Church; patron of Catholic writers and the Catholic press. Feast: January 24.)

St. Gerard Majella
Prayer for Expectant Mothers

Almighty and everlasting God, who, through the operation of the Holy Spirit, prepared the body and soul of the glorious Virgin Mary, Mother of God, to be a worthy dwelling for Your Son; who, through the same Holy Spirit, sanctified St. John the Baptist before his birth; deign to hear the prayer of Your humble servant.

Through the intercession of St. Gerard, I implore You to protect me (her) in motherhood and guard from the evil spirit the child You have given me (her), that by Your saving hand it may receive Holy Baptism.

Grant also that, having lived as good Christians on earth, both mother and child may be united in the everlasting happiness of heaven. Amen.

Prayer to St. Gerard for a Sick Child

St. Gerard, who, like our Divine Savior, showed such loving tenderness to children and delivered so many from disease and even from death, graciously look upon us now weighed down with sorrow. We implore you by your prayers to restore our child to health, if such be the holy will of God. We promise to bring him/her up a good Christian and to safeguard him/her by constant watchfulness from all contagion of sin. We implore this favor, O compassionate Brother through the love with which Jesus and Mary surrounded your own childhood. Amen.

(St. Gerard, 1726-1755, Italian Redemptorist lay brother, is known for his miracles on behalf of the poor, families, mothers and children, and those making a good confession; patron of mothers. Feast: October 16.)

St. Gertrude
Prayer for All Souls' Day

Eternal Father, I offer Thee the most precious Blood of Thy Divine Son, Jesus, in union with all the Masses said throughout the world today, for all the Holy Souls in Purgatory, for sinners everywhere, for sinners in the Universal Church, those in my own home and within my family. Amen.

(Dictated by Our Lord to St. Gertrude the Great, 1256-1302, a German mystic and writer who spread devotion to the Sacred Heart. Feast: November 16.)

St. Ignatius Loyola
For a Generous Spirit

Dearest Lord,
teach me to be generous.
Teach me to serve you as you deserve;
to give, and not to count the cost;
to fight, and not to heed the wounds;
to labor, and not to seek to rest;
to give of myself
    and not to ask for reward,
except the reward of knowing
    that I am doing your will. Amen.

(St. Ignatius, 1491-1556, founder of the Society of Jesus, the Jesuits, was a Spanish soldier who, after being wounded, converted to Christ. Feast: July 31.)

St. Jean-Baptiste Marie Vianney
How Good It Is to Love You

My Jesus, from all eternity you were pleased to give yourself to us in love. And you planted within us a deep spiritual desire that can only be satisfied by yourself. I may go from here to the other end of the world, from one country to another, from riches to greater riches, from pleasure to pleasure, and still I shall not be content. All the world cannot satisfy the immortal soul. It would be like trying to feed a starving man with a single grain of wheat. We can only be satisfied by setting our hearts, imperfect as they are, on you. We are made to love you; you created us as your lovers. It sometimes happens that the more we know a neighbor, the less we love him. But with you it is quite the opposite. The more we know you, the more we love you. Knowledge of you kindles such a fire in our souls that we have no energy left for worldly desires. My Jesus, how good it is to love you. Let me be like your disciples on Mount Tabor, seeing nothing else but you. Let us be like two bosom friends, neither of whom can ever bear to offend the other.[15]

(St. Jean-Baptiste Marie Vianney, 1786-1859, French priest, noted confessor, known as the Curé of Ars, is the patron of parish priests. Feast: August 4.)

St. John Chrysostom

O Lord and lover of the human race, shine in our hearts the pure light of your divine knowledge, and open the eyes of our mind to the understanding of your Gospel teaching.

Instill in us the fear of your blessed commandments, that, trampling upon all carnal desires, we may enter on a spiritual life, willing and doing all that is your good pleasure.

For you are the light of our souls and of our bodies, Christ, O God! And we give glory to you, together with your eternal Father and your all-holy, good, and life-giving Spirit, now and forever, world without end. Amen.

(St. John Chrysostom, c. 347-407, bishop of Constantinople, theologian, doctor of the Church known as Doctor of the Eucharist. Feast: September 13.)

Ven. John Henry Newman

Lead, kindly Light, amid th'encircling gloom,
lead thou me on!
The night is dark, and I am far from home;
lead thou me on!
Keep thou my feet; I do not ask to see
the distant scene; one step enough for me.

I was not ever thus, nor prayed that thou
shouldst lead me on;
I loved to choose and see my path; but now
lead thou me on!
I loved the garish day, and, spite of fears,
pride ruled my will: remember not past years!

So long thy power hath blessed me, sure it still
will lead me on.
O'er moor and fen, o'er crag and torrent, till
the night is gone,
And with the morn those angel faces smile,
which I have loved long since, and lost awhile!
(Amen.)

(Ven. John Henry Newman, 1801-1890, converted from the Anglican Church and became a Cardinal. He contributed to the rebirth of the Catholic Church in England.)

St. John Neumann

Father, you called John Neumann to labor for the gospel among the people of the new world. His ministry strengthened many others in the Christian faith: through his prayers may faith grow strong in this land. Grant this through our Lord Jesus Christ, your Son, who lives and reigns with you and the Holy Spirit, one God forever and ever. Amen.

(St. John Neumann, 1811-1860, bishop of Philadelphia, helped spread Forty Hours Devotion and was the first U.S. bishop to be canonized a saint. Feast: January 5.)

St. John of the Cross
Prayer for Peace

O blessed Jesus, give me stillness of soul in You. Let your mighty calmness reign in me. Rule me, O You, King of Gentleness, King of Peace.[16]

(St. John of the Cross, 1542-1591, Spanish, founder of the Discalced Carmelites and great mystical theologian and doctor of the Church, is called the Doctor of Mystical Theology. Feast: December 14.)

St. Joseph

O Glorious St. Joseph, chosen by God to be the foster-father of Jesus, the chaste spouse of Mary ever Virgin, and head of the Holy Family, be the heavenly patron and defender of the Church founded by Jesus.

With confidence we beg your powerful aid for the Church on earth. Shield it with paternal love, especially the Supreme Pontiff, together with all the bishops and priests who are in union with the Holy See. Be the defender of all who labor for souls.

Protect the working men and women and their families. Intercede for young people who are searching for their place in life. Be the sure refuge for all of us at the hour of death, and guide us safely into heaven.

In Jesus' name we pray.

Amen.

St. Joseph Novena

Loving St. Joseph, faithful follower of Jesus Christ, I raise my heart to you to implore your powerful intercession in obtaining from the Heart of Jesus all the graces necessary for my spiritual and temporal welfare, particularly the grace of a happy death, and the special grace I now implore: (mention your request here). Guardian of the Word Incarnate, I am confident that your prayers on my behalf will be graciously heard before the throne of God.

(St. Joseph, spouse of Mary our Blessed Mother and foster father of Jesus, is patron of workers and patron of a happy death. Feasts: March 19 and May 1.)

St. Jude Novena

St. Jude, glorious Apostle, faithful servant and friend of Jesus: The name of the traitor has caused you to be forgotten by many, but the Church honors and invokes you universally as the patron of difficult and desperate cases. Pray for me, I am so helpless and alone. Make use, I implore you, of that particular privilege accorded to you to bring visible and speedy help where help was almost despaired of. Come to my assistance in this great need that I may receive the consolation and help of heaven in all my necessities, tribulations, and sufferings, particularly (mention your request here), and that I may bless God with you and all the Elect throughout all eternity.

I promise you, O blessed Jude, to be ever mindful of this great favor, and I will never cease to honor you as my special and powerful patron and do all in my power to encourage devotion to you.

St. Jude, pray for us and for all who honor and invoke thy aid.

Pray three times each: Our Father, Hail Mary, and Glory Be.

(St. Jude, d. first century, was one of the Twelve Apostles and brother of St. James the Less. Martyred with Simon in Persia, he is patron of impossible and lost causes. Feast: October 28.)

Blessed Junípero Serra

God most high, your servant Junípero Serra brought the Gospel of Christ to the peoples of Mexico and California and firmly established the Church among them. By his intercession, and through the example of his evangelical zeal, inspire us to be faithful witnesses of Jesus Christ. Through the same Christ our Lord. Amen.[17]

(One of the most famous Spanish missionaries, Blessed Junípero Serra, 1713-1784, established nine of 21 Franciscan missions in California. Feast: July 1.)

Blessed Kateri Tekakwitha

O God, who, among the many marvels of your grace in the New World, did cause to blossom on the banks of the Mohawk and of the St. Lawrence, the pure and tender Lily, Kateri Tekakwitha, grant, we beseech you, the favor we beg through her intercession; that this Young Lover of Jesus and of His cross may soon be counted among her saints by Holy Mother Church, and that our hearts may be enkindled with a stronger desire to imitate her innocence and faith. Through the same Christ our Lord. Amen.[18]

(The mystic "Lily of the Mohawks," 1656-1680, was the first Native American beatified. Feast: July 14.)

St. Katharine Drexel

Ever-loving God, you called St. Katharine Drexel to teach the message of the Gospel and to bring the life of the Eucharist to the African American and Native American peoples. By her prayers and example, enable us to work for justice among the poor and oppressed, and keep us undivided in love in the Eucharistic community of your Church. We ask this through Christ our Lord. Amen.

(St. Katharine Drexel, 1858-1955, Philadelphia-born heiress, founded the Sisters of the Blessed Sacrament. Feast: March 3.)

St. Lucy Novena for Eyes

O God, our Creator and Redeemer, mercifully hear our prayers and as we venerate Your servant, St. Lucy, for the light of faith You bestowed upon her, increase and preserve this same light also to our souls, that we may be able to avoid evil, to do good, and abhor nothing so much as the blindness and the darkness of evil and of sin.

Relying on Your goodness, O God, we humbly ask You by intercession of Your servant, St. Lucy, to give perfect vision to our eyes, that they may serve for Your greater honor and glory, for our salvation and that of others, and that we may come to the enjoyment of the unfailing light of the Lamb of God in paradise.

St. Lucy, virgin and martyr, hear our prayers and obtain our petitions.

(St. Lucy, d. 304, virgin martyr of Sicily, mentioned in the First Eucharistic Prayer, endured many tortures and is invoked for eye problems. Feast: December 13.)

St. Margaret Mary Alacoque
Prayer to the Sacred Heart of Jesus

O Heart of Love,
I put all my trust in you.
For I fear all things
   from my own weakness,
but I hope for all things
   from your goodness. Amen.

(St. Margaret Mary Alacoque, 1647-1690, French religious, was instrumental in spreading the devotion to the Sacred Heart and First Friday devotions. Feast: October 16.)

St. Marguerite Bourgeoys

Marguerite Bourgeoys, you who contributed so greatly to the human and Christian promotion of the family in the New World, continue to protect our homes.

Inspire young couples to prepare in a Christian manner for marriage.

Help husbands and wives to grow in love and in fidelity to their commitments.

Assist parents in the education of their children. Obtain for them the necessary material and spiritual means to provide for their needs.

Come to the help of those whose happiness is threatened or shattered.

Bring joy to unhappy children.

Stimulate and enlighten the zeal of those who, in their respective commitments, devote themselves as you did to the human and Christian promotion of families.

Grant that we may rediscover in the Holy Family an ever living model of family life based on Gospel values, and obtain for us the protection of Jesus, Mary, and Joseph. Amen.

(St. Marguerite Bourgeoys, 1620-1700, a French nun who journeyed to Montreal, established the Secular Daughters of the Congregation de Notre Dame. Feast: January 12.)

St. Maximilian Maria Kolbe

St. Maximilian, amidst the hate and lonely misery of Auschwitz, you brought love into the lives of fellow captives and sowed the seeds of hope amidst despair. You bore witness to the world by word and deed that "Love alone creates." Help me to become more like you. With the Church and Mary and you, may I proclaim that

"Love alone creates." To the hungry and oppressed, the naked and homeless, the scorned and hated, the lonely and despairing, may I proclaim the power of Christ's love, which endures forever and ever. Amen.

(St. Maximilian Maria Kolbe, 1894-1941, Polish Conventual Franciscan, as a prisoner at Auschwitz, offered his life in exchange for another prisoner. Feast: August 14.)

Bl. Miguel Pro

I believe, O Lord; but strengthen my faith . . .
> Heart of Jesus, I love Thee; but increase my love.
> Heart of Jesus, I trust in Thee; but give greater vigor to my confidence.
> Heart of Jesus, I give my heart to Thee; but so enclose it in Thee that it may never be separated from Thee.
> Heart of Jesus, I am all Thine; but take care of my promise so that I may be able to put it in practice even unto the complete sacrifice of my life.

(Bl. Miguel Pro, 1891-1927, Mexican Jesuit, ministered to Mexican people and was executed. Feast: November 23.)

St. Odilia

O God, Who in Your kindness did give us St. Odilia, Virgin and Martyr, as the Protectress of the eyes and afflicted, grant us we humbly beseech You, to be protected, through her intercession, from the darkness of ignorance and sin and to be cured from the blindness of the eyes and other bodily infirmities. Through Him,

Who is the Light and Life of the world, Jesus Christ, Your Son, Our Lord. Amen.[19]

(St. Odilia, d.c. 720, born in Alsace, was miraculously cured of blindness at age 12; she is invoked for those with afflictions of the eyes. Feast: December 13.)

St. Patrick

May the strength of God
pilot us,
may the wisdom of God
instruct us,
may the hand of God
protect us,
may Salvation,
O Lord,
be always ours,
this day and evermore.
Amen.

(St. Patrick, 389-461, is known for his missionary work and the conversion of Ireland. Feast: March 17.)

St. Peregrine

St. Peregrine, whom Holy Mother Church has declared patron of those suffering from running sores and cancer, I confidently turn to you for aid in my present need (mention your request here).

Lest I lose confidence, I beg your kind intercession. Plead with Mary, the Mother of Sorrows, whom you loved so tenderly and in union with whom you have suffered the pains of cancer, that she may help me with her all-powerful prayers and consolation.

Obtain for me the strength to accept my trials from the loving hand of God with patience and resignation. May suffering lead me to a better life and enable me to atone for my own sins and the sins of the world.

St. Peregrine, help me to imitate you in bearing whatever cross God may permit to come to me, uniting myself with Jesus Crucified and the Mother of Sorrows. I offer my sufferings to God with all the love of my heart, for His glory and the salvation of souls, especially my own. Amen.

(St. Peregrine, 1260-1345, Italian, was received into the Order of the Servants of Mary; cancer in his foot was cured the night before he was scheduled to have it amputated. He is patron saint of cancer patients and those suffering from running sores. Feast: May 2.)

Apostles Ss. Peter and Paul

O holy Apostles Peter and Paul, intercede for us. Protect, O Lord, your people who trust in the patronage of your Apostles, Peter and Paul, and by their constant protection, protect your people. Through Christ our Lord. Amen.[20]

(Peter was the chief of the Apostles and head of the Church, the first Pope; St. Paul became the Apostle to the Gentiles through extensive missionary journeys. Feast: June 29.)

St. Richard of Chichester

Thanks be to you, my Lord Jesus Christ, for all the benefits and blessings which you have given to me, for all the pains and insults which you have borne for me. O most merciful Friend, Brother and Redeemer, may I know you more clearly, love you more dearly, and follow you more nearly.[21]

(Attributed to St. Richard of Chichester, 1198-1253, a well-educated English bishop who aided the poor and fought against corruption in the Church. Feast: April 3.)

St. Rita Novena Prayers

Holy Patroness of those in need, St. Rita, so humble, pure and patient, whose pleadings with your Divine Spouse are irresistible, obtain for us from your crucified Jesus our request. (*Mention your request here.*) Be favorable towards us for the greater glory of God and yourself, and we promise to honor and sing your praises ever afterward. Amen.

Pray three times each: Our Father, Hail Mary, and Glory Be.

+ + +

O holy protectress of those who are in utmost need, who shines as a star of hope in the midst of darkness, glorious and blessed St. Rita, bright mirror of the Catholic Church, in patience and fortitude as the patriarch Job, scourge of devils, health of the sick, deliverer of those in extreme need, admiration of saints and model of all states; with my whole heart and soul, prostrate before and firmly united to the adorable will of my God, through the merits of my only Lord and Savior Jesus Christ, and in particular of the merits of His wearing of the torturing crown of thorns, which you with a tender devotion did daily contemplate, through the merits of the most sweet Virgin Mary and your own excellent graces and virtues, I implore you to obtain my earnest petition — provided it be for the greater honor and glory of God and my own sanctification (mention your request here), and here do guide and purify my intention. O holy protectress and most dear advocate, so that I may obtain the pardon of all my sins, and grace to persevere daily as you did in walking with courage and generosity and unwavering fidelity through the heavenward path in which the love of my sweet Lord desires to lead me. Amen.

St. Rita, Advocate of the Hopeless, **pray for us.**
St. Rita, Advocate of the Impossible, **pray for us.**
Pray three times each: Our Father, Hail Mary, and Glory Be.[22]

(St. Rita, d. 1457, Italian wife and mother who became a nun upon the death of her husband and two sons, received the wounds of the Crown of Thorns and many visions. Along with St. Jude, she is patron of hopeless cases. Feast: May 22.)

St. Rose Philippine Duchesne

"You may dazzle the mind with a thousand brilliant discoveries of natural science; you may open new worlds of knowledge which were never dreamed of before; yet, if you have not developed in the soul of the pupil strong habits of virtue which will sustain him in the struggle of life, you have not educated him, but only put in his hand a powerful instrument of self-destruction."

Gracious God, you filled the heart of Rose Philippine Duchesne with charity and missionary zeal, and gave her the desire to make you known to all peoples. Fill us who honor her memory today with that same love and zeal, and extend your kingdom to the ends of the earth. We ask this through Christ our Lord. Amen.[23]

(St. Rose Philippine Duchesne, 1769-1852, a French nun and American missionary, founded the Society of the Sacred Heart. Feast: November 18.)

St. Teresa of Jesus (Ávila)
Let Nothing Disturb You

Let nothing disturb you. Let nothing frighten you. All things pass. God does not change. Patience achieves everything. Whoever has God lacks nothing. God alone suffices.

God has no body now on earth but yours; no hands but yours; no feet but yours. Yours are the eyes through which the compassion of Christ must look out on the world. Yours are the feet with which He is to go about doing good. Yours are the hands with which He is to bless His people. Amen.

(St. Teresa of Ávila, 1515-1582, Spanish Carmelite nun, was named first woman Doctor of the Church; she reformed the Carmelite Order. Feast: October 15.)

Blessed Teresa of Calcutta
Lord, Open Our Eyes

Lord, open our eyes, that we may see you in our brothers and sisters. Lord, open our ears, that we may hear the cries of the hungry, the cold, the frightened, the oppressed. Lord, open our hearts, that we may love each other as you love us. Renew in us your spirit. Lord, free us and make us one.

(Mother Teresa of Calcutta, 1910-1997, founder of Mission-aries of Charity, was thought by many to be a living saint. Her cause for beatification has begun.)

St. Thérèse of Lisieux
Five-Day Novena

St. Thérèse the Little Flower, please pick me a rose from the heavenly garden and send it to me with a message of love.

Ask God to grant me the favor I implore.

And tell Him I will love Him daily more and more.

Pray five times each: Hail Mary, Our Father, and Glory Be. If possible, the prayers should be said before 11 a.m. so there is a communion of those praying at the same time.

(St. Thérèse of Lisieux, 1873-1897, French Carmelite mystic known as the "Saint of the Little Way" or the "Little Flower," is patron of missions and a Doctor of the Church. Feast: October 1.)

St. Thomas Aquinas
For All Good Things

Loving God, who sees in us nothing that you have not given yourself, make my body healthy and agile, my mind sharp and clear, my heart joyful and contented, my soul faithful and loving. And surround me with the company of men and angels who share my devotion to you. Above all, let me live in your presence, for with you all fear is banished, and there is only harmony and peace. Let every day combine the beauty of spring, the brightness of summer, the abundance of autumn, and the repose of winter. And at the end of my life on earth, grant that I may come to see and to know you in the fullness of your glory. Amen.

(St. Thomas Aquinas, 1225-1274, was one of the Church's greatest theologians; devoted to the Blessed Sacrament, he is called the "Angelic Doctor." Feast: January 28.)

Thomas à Kempis

God, our Father, we are exceedingly frail and indisposed to every virtuous and gallant undertaking. Strengthen our weakness, we beseech you, that we may do valiantly in this spiritual war; help us against our own negligence and cowardice, and defend us from the treachery of our unfaithful hearts, for Jesus Christ's sake.

(Thomas à Kempis, 1380-1471, is alleged to have written The Imitation of Christ, *a spiritual and theological work instructing how to find spiritual perfection by imitating Christ.)*

St. Thomas More

Good Lord, give me the grace, in all my fear and agony, to have recourse to that great fear and wonderful agony that you, my sweet Savior, had at the Mount of Olivet before your most bitter passion, and in the meditation thereof, to conceive ghostly comfort and consolation profitable for my soul.

Almighty God, take from me all vainglorious minds, all appetites of mine own praise, all envy, all covetise, gluttony, sloth and lechery, all wrathful affections, all appetite of revenging, all desire or delight of other folks' harm, all pleasure in provoking any person to wrath and anger, all delight of exprobation or insultation against any persons in their affliction and calamity.

And give me, good Lord, a humble, lowly, quiet, peaceable, patient, charitable, kind, tender and pitiful mind, with all my works, and all my words, and all my thoughts, to have a taste of your Holy, Blessed Spirit.

Give me, good Lord, a full faith, a firm hope, and a fervent charity, a love to the good Lord incomparable above the love to myself; and that I love nothing to your displeasure, but everything in an order to you.

Take from me, good Lord, this lukewarm fashion, or rather key-cold manner of meditation, and this dullness in praying to you. And give me warmth, delight, and quickness in thinking of you.

And give me your grace to long for your holy sacraments, and especially to rejoice in the presence of your very blessed Body, sweet Savior Christ, in the holy sacrament of the altar, and duly to thank you for your gracious visitation therewith, and at that high memorial, with tender compassion, to remember and consider your most bitter passion. Amen.

(St. Thomas More, 1478-1535, English chancellor, suffered martyrdom for not accepting King Henry VIII's break with the Catholic Church. Feast: June 22.)

Angels

✣

Beside each believer stands an angel as protector and shepherd leading him to life.

— ST. BASIL

St. Michael the Archangel

St. Michael the Archangel, defend us in battle; be our
defense against the wickedness and snares of the devil.
May God rebuke him, we humbly pray; and do thou,
O Prince of the heavenly host, by the power of God,
thrust into hell Satan and the other evil spirits who prowl
about the world seeking the ruin of souls. Amen.

St. Raphael the Archangel

O God,
send the Archangel Raphael to our assistance.
May he who stands forever praising you
at your throne
present our humble petitions
to be blessed by you.
Through Christ our Lord. Amen.

St. Gabriel the Archangel

O God,
who from among all your angels

chose the Archangel Gabriel
to announce the mystery of the Incarnation,
mercifully grant that we
who solemnly remember him on earth
may feel the benefits of his
patronage in heaven,
who lives and reigns forever and ever. Amen.

Prayer to All the Angels

All you holy angels and archangels,
thrones and dominations,
principalities and powers,
the virtues of heaven,
cherubim and seraphim,
praise the Lord forever. Amen.

Prayers to One's Guardian Angel

Angel of God,
whom God has appointed to be my protector
    against all things evil:
be always at my side, and keep me aware of your
    presence as God's messenger to me all the days
    of my life, for my good.
Pray for me this day and every day of my life in
    this world. Amen.

+ + +

O angel of God, my guardian dear,
To whom his love commits me here,
Ever this day, be at my side,
To watch and guard, to rule and guide. Amen.

Mass

The Eucharist is "the source and summit of the Christian life."

— *SACROSANCTUM CONCILIUM,*
CONSTITUTION ON THE SACRED LITURGY

PRAYERS BEFORE MASS

Prayer by St. Thomas Aquinas

Almighty and ever-living God, /I approach the sacrament of your only-begotten Son, our Lord Jesus Christ. / I come sick to the doctor of life, /unclean to the fountain of mercy, / blind to the radiance of eternal light, /and poor and needy to the Lord of heaven and earth. /

Lord, in your great generosity, / heal my sickness, /wash away my defilement, /enlighten my blindness, /enrich my poverty, /and clothe my nakedness. / May I receive the bread of angels, /the King of kings and Lord of lords, / with humble reverence, /with the purity and faith, /with repentance and love, /and the determined purpose that will help to bring me to salvation./

May I receive the sacrament of the Lord's body and blood, /and its reality and power. / Kind God, /may I receive the body of your only-begotten Son, our Lord Jesus Christ, /born from the womb of the Virgin Mary,

/and so be received into his mystical body /and be numbered among his members.

Loving Father, /as on my earthly pilgrimage I now receive your beloved Son under the veil of a sacrament, /may I one day see him face to face in glory, /who lives and reigns with you forever and ever.

Amen.

— FROM THE SACRAMENTARY

O Sacred Banquet
By St. Thomas Aquinas

O Sacred Banquet,
in which Christ is received,
the memory of his passion is renewed,
the soul is filled with grace,
and a pledge of future glory is given to us.

Pange Lingua (Eucharistic Hymn)

Sing, my tongue, the Savior's glory,
  Of his Flesh the mystery sing;
Of the Blood, all price exceeding,
  Shed by our immortal King,
Destined for the world's redemption,
  From a noble womb to spring.

Of a pure and spotless Virgin
  Born for us on earth below,
He, as man, with man conversing,
  Stayed, the seeds of truth to sow;
Then he closed the solemn order
  Wondrously his life of woe.

On the night of that Last Supper
  Seated with his chosen band,
He, the Pascal Victim eating,
  First fulfills the Law's command:
Then as Food to all his brethren
  Gives himself with his own hand.

Word made flesh, the bread of nature
  By his word to Flesh he turns;
Wine into his Blood he changes:
  What though sense no change discerns?
Only be the heart in earnest,
  Faith her lesson quickly learns.

Tantum Ergo

Down in adoration falling,
  Lo! the Sacred Host we hail;
Lo! o'er ancient forms departing,
  Newer rites of grace prevail;
Faith for all defects supplying
  Where the feeble sense fail.

To the everlasting Father,
  And the Son who reigns on high,
With the Holy Spirit proceeding
  Forth from each eternally,
Be salvation, honor, blessing,
  Might, and endless majesty. Amen.

Spiritual Communion

When unable to receive Holy Communion, the following prayer of St. Francis may be used:

I believe that you, O Jesus, are in the most holy Sacrament. I love you and desire you. Come into my heart. I embrace You. O, never leave me. May the burning and most sweet power of your love, O Lord Jesus Christ, I beseech you, absorb my mind that I may die through love of your love, Who were graciously pleased to die through love of my love.

PRAYERS AFTER COMMUNION

Jesus, my Lord, my God, my all, I hold you within my living breast; the same Jesus who so often rested on the breast of His mother.

Sacrament of my God, my Jesus, my life and my love, how I love to be with you. How necessary you are to my heart! How sweet and tender are the sentiments you excite in my soul! God of love, divine object of all earthly happiness, what peace I enjoy when near you. What holy joy, even in the midst of troubles and sorrows of my offenses. Before you the universe is in a profound silence. Before you all things are as nothing to me. You alone, O my Jesus, are all to me.

— ADAPTED FROM A PRAYER BY
ST. CATHERINE OF GENOA

Prayer for Holiness

O Lord Jesus Christ, Son of the living God, Who, by the will of the Father, with the cooperation of the Holy Spirit, have by Your death given life to the world, deliver me by this Your Most Sacred Body and Blood from all sins and from every evil. Make me always cling to Your commandments, and never permit me to be separated from You. Who with the same God the Father and the Holy Spirit, live and reign, God, world without end. Amen.

PRAYERS AFTER MASS

Anima Christi (Soul of Christ)

Soul of Christ, sanctify me;
Body of Christ, save me;
Blood of Christ, drench me;
Water from the side of Christ, wash me.
Passion of Christ, strengthen me.
O good Jesus, hear me;
Within your wounds hide me;
Never permit me to be separated from you;
From the wicked enemy defend me;
In the hour of my death call me
And bid me come to your side,
That with your saints I may praise you,
Forever and ever. Amen.

— ATTRIBUTED BY SOME TO
BL. BERNARDINE OF FELTRE

Prayer to Christ Crucified

Look down upon me,
good and gentle Jesus,
while before your face I humbly kneel
and with burning affection
I pray and beg you to fix deep in my heart
lively sentiments of faith, hope, and love,
true contrition for my sins,

and a firm purpose of amendment.
I contemplate with great love and pity
your five most precious wounds,
pondering over them within me,
while I call to mind
the words which David the prophet
said concerning you, my Jesus:
"They have pierced my hands and my feet;
they have numbered all my bones."

Look with Mercy

O God, our refuge and our strength, look down with mercy upon the people who cry to Thee; and by the intercession of the glorious and immaculate Virgin Mary, Mother of God, of St. Joseph her spouse, of the blessed Apostles Peter and Paul, and of all the saints, in Thy mercy and goodness hear our prayers for the conversion of sinners, and for the liberty and exaltation of the Holy Mother Church. Through the same Christ Our Lord. Amen.

Prayer by St. Thomas Aquinas

Lord, Father all-powerful and ever-living God, /I thank you, /for even though I am a sinner, your unprofitable servant, /not because of my worth but in the kindness of your mercy, /you have fed me with the precious body and blood of your Son, our Lord /Jesus Christ.

I pray that this Holy Communion / may not bring me condemnation and punishment, / but forgiveness and salvation.

May it be a helmet of faith /and a shield of good will.

May it purify me from evil ways /and put an end to my evil passions.

May it bring me charity and patience, /humility and obedience, /and growth in the power to do good.

May it be my strong defense /against all my enemies, visible and invisible, /And the perfect calming of all my evil impulses, / bodily and spiritual.

May it unite me more closely to you, /the one true God, /and lead me safely through death /to everlasting happiness with you.

And I pray that you will lead me, a sinner, /to the banquet where you, /with your Son and Holy Spirit, /are true and perfect light, /total fulfillment, everlasting joy, /gladness without end, /and perfect happiness to your saints.

Grant this through Christ our Lord. Amen.

— From the Sacramentary

Universal Prayer by Pope Clement XI

Lord, I believe in you: increase my faith.
　I trust in you: strengthen my trust.
　I love you: let me love you more and more.
　I am sorry for my sins: deepen my sorrow.

I worship you as my first beginning,
　I long for you as my last end.
　I praise you as my constant helper,
　　and call on you as my loving protector.

Guide me by your wisdom,
　correct me with your justice,
　comfort me with your mercy,
　protect me with your power.

I offer you, Lord,
　my thoughts: to be fixed on you;
　my words: to have you for their theme;

my actions: to reflect my love for you;
my sufferings: to be endured for your greater
glory.

I want to do what you ask of me:
in the way you ask,
for as long as you ask,
because you ask it.

Lord, enlighten my understanding,
strengthen my will,
purify my heart,
and make me holy.

Help me to repent of my past sins
and to resist temptation in the future.
Help me to rise above my human weaknesses
and to grow stronger as a Christian.

Let me love you, my Lord and my God,
to see myself as I really am:
a pilgrim in this world,
a Christian called to respect and love
all those whose lives I touch,
those in authority over me,
my friends and my enemies.

Help me to conquer anger with gentleness,
greed by generosity,
apathy by fervor.
Help me to forget myself and reach out to others.

Make me prudent in planning,
courageous in taking risks,
patient in suffering,
unassuming in prosperity.

Keep me, Lord, attentive at prayer,
  temperate in food and drink,
  diligent in my work,
  and firm in my intentions.

Let my conscience be clear,
  my conduct without fault,
  my speech blameless,
  my life well-ordered.

Put me on guard against my human weaknesses.
  Let me cherish your love for me,
  keep your law,
  and come at last to your salvation.

Teach me to be aware that this world is passing,
  that my true future is the happiness of heaven,
  that life on earth is short,
  and the life to come eternal.

Help me to prepare for death with a proper fear of
    judgment,
  but a greater trust in your goodness.
  Lead me safely through death
  to the endless joys of heaven.

Grant this through Christ our Lord. Amen.

Eucharistic Adoration

Oh! Yes, Lord Jesus, come and reign! Let my body be Your temple, my heart Your throne, my will Your devoted servant; let me be Yours forever, living only in You and for you!

— St. Peter Julian Eymard

O Sacrament most holy, O Sacrament divine!
All praise and all thanksgiving be every
   moment Thine!

Short Visit to the Blessed Sacrament

I place myself in the presence of Him, in whose Incarnate Presence I am before I place myself there.

I adore You, O my Savior, present here as God and man, in soul and body, in true flesh and blood.

I acknowledge and confess that I kneel before the Sacred Humanity, which was conceived in Mary's womb, and lay in Mary's bosom; which grew up to man's estate, and by the Sea of Galilee called the Twelve, wrought miracles, and spoke words of wisdom and peace; which in due season hung on the cross, lay in the tomb, rose from the dead, and now reigns in heaven.

I praise and bless, and give myself wholly to Him,
Who is the true Bread of my soul, and my everlasting joy.

— VEN. JOHN HENRY NEWMAN

Before the Blessed Sacrament

O most Holy Trinity, Father, Son, and Holy Spirit, I
adore you profoundly. I offer you the most precious
body, blood, soul and divinity of Jesus Christ, present
in all the tabernacles of the world, in reparation for the
outrages, sacrileges and indifferences by which He is
offended. By the infinite merits of the Sacred Heart of
Jesus and the Immaculate Heart of Mary, I beg the conversion of sinners.

— PRAYER FROM THE FÁTIMA CHILDREN

Act When Visiting the Most
Holy Sacrament

My Lord Jesus Christ, who, for the love you bear to
mankind, do remain night and day in this Sacrament,
full of pity and love, awaiting, calling, and receiving all
who come to visit you; I believe that you are present in
the Sacrament of the Altar; I adore you from the depths
of my own nothingness; I thank you for the many graces
you have given me, and especially for having given me
yourself in this Sacrament; for having given me Mary
your Mother as my advocate, and for having called me
to visit you in this church.

— ST. ALPHONSUS LIGUORI

Prayers throughout the Day

✢

Prayer is the life of the new heart. It ought to animate us at every moment.

— *Catechism of the Catholic Church,*
no. 2697

MORNING PRAYERS

(Basic prayers may be used, including the Our Father; Hail Mary; Glory Be; Acts of Faith, Hope and Charity; the Apostles' Creed; and others.)

Morning Offering

O Jesus, through the Immaculate Heart of Mary, I offer you all my prayers, works, joys and sufferings of this day, for all the intentions of your Sacred Heart, in union with the Holy Sacrifice of the Mass throughout the world, in reparation for my sins, for the intentions of all my relatives and friends and in particular for the intentions of the Holy Father.

Daily Intentions

(May be used following the Morning Offering.)

Sunday: To obtain a true spirit of zeal, religion, and piety. For the success of priests' work and the spiritual welfare of those entrusted to their care.

Monday: Spirit of meekness and humility. Souls in purgatory and for Religious communities.

Tuesday: Spirit of Faith. Relatives, friends, and benefactors.

Wednesday: Spirit of Charity. The sick, dying, suffering, poor, and those who care for them.

Thursday: Love of the Holy Eucharist. Vocations to the Priesthood; conversion of unbelievers; needs of missionaries.

Friday: Spirit of mortification and self-sacrifice. Conversion of sinners.

Saturday: Love of chastity and of the Blessed Virgin. Schools and teachers; children and youth.

(Add your own private intentions to those suggested above.)[24]

A Morning Prayer

O Jesus,
I offer you my prayers, works, joys, and sufferings of this day.
I join myself to all your people,
in praying for the salvation of souls,
    the reunion of all Christians,
       the grace of repentance,
         and the intentions of our Holy Father.

I wish to make my life this day
a prayer on behalf of _____ . Amen.

A Morning or Evening Prayer

Lord Jesus, I give you my hands to do your work. I give you my feet to go your way. I give you my eyes to see as you see. I give you my tongue to speak your words. I give you my mind to think as you think. I give you my spirit so that you may pray in me. I give you my self so that you may grow in me. So that it is you, Lord Jesus, who lives and works and prays in me. Amen.[25]

Confidence in God

By St. Francis de Sales

My God, I give you this day. I offer you, now, all of the good that I shall do and I promise to accept, for love of you, all of the difficulty that I shall meet. Help me to conduct myself during this day in a manner pleasing to you. Amen.

Prayer of Pope Paul VI

Make us worthy, Lord, to serve our fellow men throughout the world who live and die in poverty and hunger. Give them, through our hands this day, their daily bread, and by our understanding love, give peace and joy. Amen.

PRAYERS DURING THE DAY

(Other prayers that may be used include: Memorare; *Hail Holy Queen; Angel of God; St. Michael the Archangel; the Rosary; and the Chaplet of Divine Mercy, among others.)*

Aspirations

Short prayers that may be said throughout the day during work or play as you raise your ordinary actions to God.

Lord, help me.

May Jesus Christ be praised.

Jesus, mercy!

Lord, I believe in You.

Lord, I adore You.

Lord, I place my trust in You.

I love You, my God.

Jesus, I love You.

All for You, most Sacred Heart of Jesus.

Your will be done.

As the Lord wills.

O God, help me.

Comfort me, my Jesus.

Graciously hear my prayer, O Lord.

My Jesus, save me.

My God and my all.

O God, have mercy on me, a sinner.

O Lord, increase our faith.

My Lord and my God.

Stay with us, O Lord.

Mother of Sorrows, pray for us.

Jesus, Mary, Joseph, I love you; save souls.
O Most Blessed Trinity, I adore You.

The Jesus Prayer

From early Christian monasticism, simple but intense meditation was encouraged. It consists of repeating one of the following from Scripture or similar forms over and over:

Jesus Christ, Son of God, have mercy on us!

Lord Jesus, Son of the living God, have mercy on me a sinner!

O Lord Jesus Christ, have mercy on me, a sinner!

The Angelus

V. The angel of the Lord declared unto Mary;
R. And she conceived by the Holy Spirit.
Hail, Mary . . .

V. Behold the handmaid of the Lord.
R. Be it done unto me according to your word.
Hail, Mary . . .

V. And the Word was made flesh,
R. And dwelt among us.
Hail, Mary . . .

V. Pray for us, O holy Mother of God,
R. That we may be made worthy of the promises of Christ.
Let us pray.
Pour forth, we beseech you, O Lord, your grace into our hearts, that we, to whom the incarnation of Christ, your Son, was made known by the message

of an angel, may by his passion and cross be brought to the glory of his resurrection, through the same Christ our Lord.

R. Amen.

(The Angelus is traditionally prayed at 6 a.m., noon, and 6 p.m.)

Acceptance of God's Will

In all things may the most holy, the most just, and the most lovable will of God be done, praised, and exalted above all forever. Your will be done, O Lord, your will be done. The Lord has given, and the Lord has taken away; blessed be the name of the Lord now and always. Amen.[26]

MEALTIME PRAYERS

Grace before Meals

Bless us, O Lord, and these thy gifts
    which we are about to receive
    from thy bounty.
Through Christ Our Lord. Amen.

Many add the following verse:

May the souls of the faithful departed,
    through the mercy of God,
    rest in peace. Amen.

Prayer after Meals

We give you thanks for all your gifts,
almighty God,
    living and reigning now and forever. Amen.

Blessing of Bread

O Lord Jesus Christ, bread of angels, living bread
unto eternal life, bless this bread as you did bless the five
loaves in the wilderness; that all who eat it with reverence may through it attain the corporal and spiritual
health they desire. You live and reign eternally. Amen.

EVENING AND NIGHT PRAYERS

Prayer at Coming Home Each Day

Hear us, Lord,
    and send your angel from heaven
    to visit and protect,
    to comfort and defend
    all who live in this house.[27]

The *Magnificat* or Canticle of Mary
(Luke 1:46-55)

My soul magnifies the Lord,
    and my spirit rejoices in God my savior;
    for he has regarded the low estate of his
        handmaiden.
For behold, henceforth all generations will call
    me blessed:

for he who is mighty has done great things
   for me,
and holy is his name.

And his mercy is on those who fear him
   from generation to generation.

He has shown strength with his arm,
   he has scattered the proud in the
      imagination of their hearts,

He has put down the mighty from their thrones,
   and exalted those of low degree;

he has filled the hungry with good things,
   and the rich he has sent empty away.

He has helped his servant Israel
   in remembrance of his mercy,
   as he spoke to our fathers,
   to Abraham and to his posterity forever.

Prayer in the Evening
Attributed to St. Augustine

Watch, O Lord, with those who wake, or watch, or
   weep tonight,
And give Your angels and saints charge over those
   who sleep.
Tend Your sick ones, O Lord Christ;
Rest Your weary ones;
Bless Your dying ones:
Soothe Your suffering ones;
Pity Your afflicted ones;
Shield Your joyous ones;
And all for Your love's sake. Amen.

Night Prayers

Now I lay me down to sleep,
I pray the Lord my soul to keep.
Four corners to my bed,
Four angels there aspread:
Two to foot and two to head,
And four to carry me when I'm dead.

If any danger come to me,
Sweet Jesus Christ, deliver me.
And if I die before I wake,
I pray the Lord my soul to take.

God bless N.
God bless N. Amen.

✝ ✝ ✝

Angel sent by God to guide me,
be my light and walk beside me;
be my guardian and protect me;
on the paths of life direct me.[28]

Act of Contrition

O my God, I am heartily sorry for having offended you,
and I detest all my sins, because of your just punish-
ments, but most of all because they offend you, my God,
who are all good and deserving of all my love. I firmly
resolve, with the help of your grace, to sin no more and
to avoid the near occasions of sin. Amen.

*(Use during the Sacrament of Reconciliation and after a
nightly examination of conscience.)*

Everyday Prayers

✜

For me, prayer is a surge of the heart; it is a simple look turned toward heaven, it is a cry of recognition and of love, embracing both trial and joy.

— St. Thérèse of Lisieux

Prayer for a Family

Lord, bless our family, all of us now together, those far away, all who are gone back to you. May we know joy. May we bear our sorrows in patience. Let love guide our understanding of each other. Let us be grateful to each other. We have all made each other what we are. O Family of Jesus, watch over our family. Amen.[29]

Prayer for Those We Love

Lord God, we can hope for others nothing better than the happiness we desire for ourselves. Therefore, I pray you, do not separate me after death from those I tenderly loved on earth. Grant that where I am they may be with me, and that I may enjoy their presence in heaven after being so often deprived of it on earth. Lord God, I ask you to receive your beloved children immediately into your life-giving heart. After this brief life on earth, give them eternal happiness. Amen.[30]

— St. Ambrose of Milan

Prayer by Lancelot Andrewes

Remember, O Lord, infants, children, the growing youths, the young men and women, the middle-aged, the old, the decayed; hungry, thirsty, naked, sick, captive and friendless strangers; those possessed with devils and tempted to suicide; those troubled by unclean spirits; the sick in soul or body; the fainthearted, the despairing; those in prisons and chains, and all under the sentence of death; orphans, widows, foreigners, travelers, voyagers; women with child, women with child at breast; those in bitter servitude, those who work in mines, and those who suffer loneliness. Amen.

Prayer to Be Generous

Thank you, dear God, for all the things that you have given me: family, food, clothing, and home. You have given me health, a mind, and free will. Best of all, dear God, you have given me the gift of true faith. Help me to share with others the love you give to me. Amen.[31]

Prayer for Welcoming Guests

May grace be yours
and peace in abundance from God,
now and forever.
R. Amen.

Prayer for Friends
(An old French Prayer)

Blessed Mother of those whose names you can read in my heart, watch over them with every care. Make their way easy and their labors fruitful. Dry their tears if they weep; sanctify their joys; raise their courage if they weaken; restore their hope if they lose heart, their health if they be ill, truth if they err, and repentance if they fall. Amen.

Prayer for One's Enemies

Almighty God, have mercy on N. and on all that bear me evil will and would do me harm, and on their faults and mine together, by such easy, tender, merciful means, as Thine infinite wisdom best can devise; vouchsafe to amend and redress and make us saved souls in heaven together, where we may ever live and love together with thee and thy blessed saints. O glorious Trinity, for the bitter passion of our sweet Savior, Christ. Amen.

— ST. THOMAS MORE (1478-1535)

Thanksgiving for a Safe Return

Praise to you, O Lord, for our safe return.
In your great mercy,
    continue to guide and protect us
    and keep us safe. Amen.

Motorists' Prayer

Lord, protect me, my passengers, and all who I pass by with a steady hand and a watchful eye.

An Old Gaelic Blessing

May the road rise to meet you.
May the wind be always at your back.
May the sun shine warm upon your face.
May the rains fall softly upon your fields.
And, until we meet again, may God hold you in
the hollow of His hand.

Blessing from the Book of Numbers 6:24-26

The Lord bless you and keep you!
The Lord smile upon you and be gracious to you!
The Lord look upon you kindly and give you
peace!

In Thanksgiving for a Favor Received

Thank you, O God, for hearing my prayer and granting my request. Thank You for all the kindness You have shown me.

Thank you, Father, for Your great love in giving me my life, for Your great patience in preserving me despite my sinfulness, for Your protection in the past and for the opportunity to serve and honor You in the future.

Thank you, Lord Jesus, for keeping me numberless times from sin and death by the toils of Your life, the sufferings of Your Passion, and by Your victorious Resurrection.

Thank you, Holy Spirit of God, for bestowing so many graces upon my soul and for having so frequently renewed Your life within me.

May my life, from now on, be a sign of my gratefulness. Amen.[32]

Serenity Prayer

God grant me the *serenity* to accept the things I
cannot change . . .
The *courage* to change the things I can . . .
And the *wisdom* to know the difference.

Prayer to St. Joseph, Patron of Workers
Pope St. Pius X

Glorious St. Joseph, patron of all who are devoted to
toil, obtain for me the grace to toil in the spirit of
penance, in order thereby to atone for my many sins.

To toil conscientiously, putting devotion to duty
before my own inclinations.

To labor with thankfulness and joy, deeming it an
honor to employ and to develop, by my labor, the gifts
I have received from Almighty God.

To work, above all, with a pure intention and with
detachment from self, having always before my eyes the
hour of death and the accounting which I must then render of time ill-spent, of talents unemployed, of good
undone and of my empty pride in success, which is so
fatal to the work of God.

All for Jesus, all through Mary, all in imitation of
thee, O Patriarch Joseph! This shall be my motto in
life and in death. Amen.

Blessing of New Fruits

We thank you, O God, and offer you the first fruits you
have given us to enjoy, that have been produced by your
word, bidding the earth to bring forth all kinds of fruits,
to refresh and feed mankind and all the beasts.

We praise you, O God, for all these gifts and for all the benefits you have bestowed on us, adorning all creation with diverse fruits, through your Son, Jesus Christ our Lord, through whom you are glorified forever and ever. Amen.

— ADAPTED FROM A PRAYER USED IN THE FOURTH CENTURY

Prayer for Guidance

Lord, grant that I may always allow myself to be guided by you, always follow your plans and perfectly accomplish your holy will. Grant that in all things, great and small, today and all the days of my life, I may do whatever you require of me. Help me respond to the slightest prompting of your grace so that I may be your trustworthy instrument for your honor. May your will be done in time and in eternity — by me, in me, and through me. Amen.

— ST. TERESA OF ÁVILA

Prayer before Study

Let us pray. Direct, O Lord, we beseech you, all our actions by your holy inspirations, and carry them on by your gracious assistance, that every prayer and work of ours may begin always from you, and by you be happily ended. Through Christ our Lord. Amen. *Hail Mary, Glory Be.*[33]

Pilgrim's Prayer

Along ways of peace and prosperity may the almighty and merciful Lord lead us, and may the Angel Raphael accompany us on the journey. So may we in peace, health, and joy return unto our own.

Prayer to Avert Storms

Let all the winds of evil be driven from your house, we implore you, O Lord, and may the raging tempests be subdued, through our Lord Jesus Christ, your Son, who lives and reigns with you in the unity of the Holy Spirit, world without end. Amen.[34]

Lady of this House

Mary, conceived without sin, I have recourse to you. May Jesus Christ be praised.

Holy Mary, Virgin Mother of God, who was conceived without sin, I choose you this day as the Lady and mistress of this house. I ask you through your Immaculate Conception, to preserve it from pestilence, fire, and floods, from lightning and tempest, from earthquakes and sudden death. Bless and protect, O holy Mary, all who live here. Obtain for them the graces to avoid all sins, and save them from misfortune and accident.

Praised be Jesus Christ.

And the Word made flesh and dwelt among us! Praised forever be the Holy Sacrament of the Altar! "In you, O Lord, I put my trust; let me ever confide in you."

Bless Our Work

Bless, O Lord of the centuries and the millennia, the daily work by which men and women provide bread for themselves and their loved ones. We also offer to your fatherly hands the toil and sacrifices associated with work, in union with your Son Jesus Christ, who redeemed human work from the yoke of sin and restored it to its original dignity.

— POPE JOHN PAUL II

Stations of the Cross
or Way of the Cross

After an introductory prayer, each station usually begins with:

V. We adore you, O Christ, and we praise you.
R. Because by your holy Cross you have redeemed the world.

At each station, a meditation is made and a prayer may be added. Suggested texts appear after the stations. In public devotions a verse of the Stabat Mater *(see page 33) is often sung after each station.*

The First Station: Jesus is condemned to death. (Mt. 27:26; Mk. 15:15; Lk. 23:23-25; Jn. 19:16)

The Second Station: Jesus is made to carry the Cross. (Jn. 19:17)

The Third Station: Jesus falls the first time. (Mt. 27:31)

The Fourth Station: Jesus meets his Blessed Mother. (Jn. 19:25-27)

The Fifth Station: Simon helps Jesus carry his Cross. (Mt. 27:32; Mk. 15:21; Lk. 23:26)

The Sixth Station: Veronica wipes the face of Jesus. (Lk. 23:27)

The Seventh Station: Jesus falls the second time. (Lk. 23:26)

The Eighth Station: Jesus speaks to the women of Jerusalem. (Lk. 23:28-31)

The Ninth Station: Jesus falls the third time. (Jn. 19:17)

The Tenth Station: Jesus is stripped of his garments. (Lk. 23:34)

The Eleventh Station: Jesus is nailed to the Cross. (Mt. 27:33-38; Mk. 15:22-27; Lk. 23:33-34; Jn. 19:18)

The Twelfth Station: Jesus dies on the Cross. (Mt. 27:46-50; Mk. 15:34-37; Lk. 23:46; Jn. 19:28-30)

The Thirteenth Station: Jesus is taken down from the Cross. (Mt. 27:57-58; Mk. 15:42-45; Lk. 28:50-52; Jn. 19:38)

The Fourteenth Station: Jesus is placed in the tomb. (Mt. 27:59-61; Mk. 15:46-47; Lk. 23:53-56; Jn. 19:39-42)

The Fifteenth Station (optional): The Resurrection. (Mt 28; Mk. 16; Lk. 24; Jn. 20)

The Stations are usually conducted with prayers for the intentions of the Holy Father, e.g., an Our Father, Hail Mary, and Glory Be.

(The Stations of the Cross is an ancient devotion brought back from the Holy Land, where pilgrims retraced the footsteps of Jesus on the road to Calvary.)

Prayer in Time of Sickness

O Jesus, You suffered and died for us;
You understand suffering;

Teach me to understand my suffering as You do;
To bear it in union with You;
To offer it with You to atone for my sins
And to bring Your grace to souls in need.
Calm my fears; increase my trust,
May I gladly accept Your holy will and become
more like You in trial.
If it be Your will, restore me to health so that I may
work for Your honor and glory and the salvation
of all. Amen.[35]

Prayer for the Sick

Father,
your Son accepted our sufferings
to teach us the virtue of patience in
human illness.
Hear the prayers we offer for our sick brother/sister.
May all who suffer pain, illness or disease
realize that they are chosen to be saints,
and know that they are joined to Christ
in His suffering for the salvation of the world,
who lives and reigns with you and
the Holy Spirit,
one God, for ever and ever.
Amen.

— FROM THE SACRAMENTARY

Prayers of Those Who Are Sick

Those who are sick may use short prayers, repeated slowly over and over.

Lord Jesus Christ,
Son of the living God,
have mercy on me.
Praised be Jesus Christ.
Lord, I hope in you.
Your will be done.
Strengthen me, Lord.
Lord, have mercy.
Sacred Heart of Jesus, have mercy on us.
My Lord and my God.
Jesus, Mary, and Joseph.
Pray for us, holy Mother of God,
that we may become worthy of the promises of
    Christ.
Holy Mary, pray for us.[36]

Prayer for the Departed

V. Eternal rest grant unto them, O Lord,
R. and let perpetual light shine upon them.

V. May they rest in peace.
R. Amen.

V. May their souls and the souls of all the faithful
    departed, through the mercy of God, rest in
    peace.
R. Amen.[37]

Prayer to St. Joseph for a Happy Death

O Blessed Joseph, who died in the arms of Jesus and
Mary, obtain for me, I beseech you, the grace of a happy
death. In that hour of dread and anguish, assist me by
your presence, and protect me by your power against the

enemies of my salvation. Into your sacred hands, living and dying, Jesus, Mary, Joseph, I commend my soul. Amen.

The *Nunc Dimittis*

Lord, now let your servant go in peace;
  your word has been fulfilled:
my own eyes have seen the salvation
  which you have prepared in the sight of
    every people:
a light to reveal you to the nations
  and the glory of your people Israel.
    (See Lk. 2:29-32.)

Prayers after Death
Antiphons of Commendation

May the Angels lead you to paradise;
may the martyrs come to welcome you
and take you to the new city,
the new and eternal Jerusalem.

+ + +

May choirs of angels welcome you
and lead you to the bosom of Abraham;
and where Lazarus is poor no longer
may you find eternal rest.

+ + +

Whoever believes in me,
even though that person die, shall live.
R. I am the resurrection and the life.
Whoever lives and believes in me will never die.**R.**[38]

Prayer for the Bereaved

Father of mercies and God of all consolation,
you pursue us with untiring love
and dispel the shadow of death
with the bright dawn of life.

Comfort your family in their loss and sorrow,
Be our refuge and our strength, O Lord,
and lift us from the depths of grief
into the peace and light of your presence.

Your Son, our Lord Jesus Christ,
by dying has destroyed our death,
and by rising, restored our life.
Enable us therefore to press on toward him,
so that, after our earthly course is run,
he may reunite us with those we love,
when every tear will be wiped away.

We ask this through Christ our Lord.
R. Amen.[39]

Prayers for the Church and the World

The Church is a sacrament of salvation for all mankind.

— POPE JOHN PAUL II,
REDEMPTORIS MISSIO, NO. 20

Prayer for All

O Lord, Jesus Christ, hear my prayers for our Holy Father, our Bishop, our clergy, and for all who are in authority over us. Bless the whole Catholic Church, and turn all hearts toward your most merciful Heart. Bless my relatives, benefactors, friends and enemies. Help the poor, the sick, and those who are in their last agony. Have compassion on the souls in purgatory: grant them eternal rest and peace. Amen.

Prayer for Christian Unity
(Ut unum sint)

Lord Jesus Christ, at your Last Supper you prayed to the Father that all should be one. Send your Holy Spirit upon all who hear your name and seek to serve you. Strengthen our faith in you, and lead us to love one another in humility. May we who have been reborn in one baptism be united in one faith under one Shepherd. Amen.[40]

Prayer Attributed to Pope St. Leo the Great
(Pope from 440-461)

Against Error

O God, you who have established the foundations of your Church upon the holy mountains: Grant that she may not be moved by any wiles of error which would fain compass her overthrow, nor may she be shaken by any earthly disquietude, but ever stand firmly upon the ordinances of the Apostles, and by their help, be kept in safety.[41]

Prayer for the Pope

Father of providence,
look with love on our Holy Father, Pope N.,
your appointed successor to St. Peter
on whom you built your Church.
May he be the visible center and foundation
of our unity in faith and love.
Grant this through our Lord Jesus Christ, your
     Son,
who lives and reigns with you and the Holy Spirit,
one God, forever and ever. Amen.

Lord,
source of eternal life and truth,
give to your shepherd, N.,
a spirit of courage and right judgment,
a spirit of knowledge and love.
By governing with fidelity those entrusted to his care

may he, as the successor to the apostle Peter and Vicar
of Christ,
build your Church into a sacrament of unity, love,
and peace for all the world.
We ask this through our Lord Jesus Christ, your Son,
who lives and reigns with you and the Holy Spirit,
one God, forever and ever. Amen.

— FROM THE SACRAMENTARY

*(It is a mark of Catholic unity to be devoted to the Pope
and to pray for him and his intentions regularly.)*

Prayer for a Bishop

Lord our God,
you have chosen your servant N.
to be a shepherd of your flock
in the tradition of the apostles.
Give him a spirit of courage and right judgment,
a spirit of knowledge and love.
By governing with fidelity those entrusted to his care
may he build your Church as a sign of salvation for the
world.
We ask this through our Lord Jesus Christ, your Son,
who lives and reigns with you and the Holy Spirit,
one God, for ever and ever. Amen.

— FROM THE SACRAMENTARY

Prayer for Priests

O holy Mother of God, pray for the priests your Son has
chosen to serve the Church. Help them, by your intercession, to be holy, zealous, and chaste. Make them mod-
els of virtue in the service of God's people.

Help them be pious in meditation, efficacious in
preaching, and zealous in the daily offering of the Holy

Sacrifice of the Mass. Help them administer the sacraments with joy. Amen.

— St. Charles Borromeo

Prayer for Vocations to the Priesthood

Lord Jesus Christ, Shepherd of souls, who called the apostles to be fishers of men, raise up new apostles in your holy Church. Teach them that to serve you is to reign: to possess you is to possess all things. Kindle in the hearts of our people the fire of zeal for souls. Make them eager to spread your Kingdom upon earth. Grant them courage to follow you, who are the Way, the Truth and the Life; who lives and reigns forever and ever. Amen.[42]

Prayer for One's Vocation in Life

Lord, make me a better person: more considerate toward others, more honest with myself, more faithful to you. Help me to find my true vocation in life and grant that through it I may find happiness myself and bring happiness to others. Grant, Lord, that those whom you call to enter priesthood or religious life may have the generosity to answer your call, so that those who need your help may always find it. We ask this through Christ our Lord. Amen.[43]

Prayer for the Missions

O God, who would have all His children to be saved and to come to the knowledge of the truth, send forth, we beseech you, laborers into your harvest and grant them with all confidence to preach the Word; that everywhere your Gospel may be heard and glorified, and that all nations may know you, the one True God, and Him whom you have sent, Jesus Christ, your Son, our Lord. Amen.[44]

Prayer for Conversions

(May be recited daily in September for the success of R.C.I.A. or inquiry classes.)

O Blessed Apostle, St. Paul, greatest of all converts, who labored unceasingly for the conversion of other souls, inspire me with the ardor of your zeal that I may pray and work for the conversion of my brethren, redeemed in the Blood of Christ but not as yet blessed with the full light of His Truth. Mindful of the loving concern of the Divine Shepherd for the salvation of the "other sheep that are not of this fold," I now beg your intercession to obtain the grace of conversion for (name of family member, friend or others). May God, the Holy Spirit from Whom alone this gift can come, hear my humble prayer and thus enable me to share with others the riches of my heritage of faith through Jesus Christ, Our Lord. Amen.[45]

Prayer for America

We pray to Thee, O God of might, wisdom and justice, through whom authority is rightly administered, laws are enacted, and judgments decreed, assist with Thy holy Spirit of counsel and fortitude the President of the United States, that his administration may be conducted in righteousness, and be eminently useful to Thy people over whom he presides, by encouraging due respect for virtue and religion, by a faithful execution of the laws in justice and mercy, and by restraining vice and immorality.

Let the light of Thy divine wisdom direct the deliberations of Congress and shine forth in all the proceedings and laws framed for our rule and government, so that they may tend to the preservation of peace, the promotion of national happiness, the increase of industry, sobriety, and useful knowledge; and may perpetuate to us the blessings of equal liberty.

— BISHOP JOHN CARROLL

(In 1789, Father John Carroll was named the first American bishop to the Diocese of Baltimore, which then encompassed the entire United States.)

Prayer to St. Gerard Majella for the Pro-Life Movement

St. Gerard Majella, women the world over have adopted you as their patron in the joys and fears of childbearing. Today, we invoke your intercession for the pro-life movement. Pray that all will look upon human life as a great gift from God to be accepted and loved, not as an unwanted burden to be destroyed. Assist from heaven the efforts of those on earth who are enlisted in the Christlike crusade of promoting the dignity and value of all human life, particularly the unborn. This we ask through Christ, our Lord. Amen.

Pope John Paul II's Prayer for Life

O Mary,
bright dawn of the new world,
Mother of the living,
to you do we entrust the *cause of life*:

Look down, O Mother,
upon the vast numbers

of babies not allowed to be born,
of the poor whose lives are made difficult,
of men and women who are
victims of brutal violence,
of the elderly and the sick killed
by indifference or out of misguided mercy.

Grant that all who believe in your Son
may *proclaim the Gospel of life*
with honesty and love
to the people of our time.

Obtain for them the grace
to *accept that Gospel*
as a gift ever new,
the joy of *celebrating it* with gratitude
throughout their lives
and the courage to *bear witness to it*
resolutely, in order to build,
together with all people of good will,
the civilization of truth and love,
to the praise and glory of God,
the Creator and lover of life.

— *Evangelium Vitae*, no. 105.4

Prayer for Peace

God of perfect peace, / violence and cruelty can have no
part with you. / May those who are at peace with one
another / hold fast to the good will that unites them; /
may those who are enemies forget their hatred / and be
healed. /We ask this through our Lord Jesus Christ, your
Son, / who lives and reigns with you and the Holy Spirit,
/ one God, forever and ever. Amen.

— FROM THE SACRAMENTARY

Sacred Scripture

✠

Ignorance of the Scriptures is ignorance of Christ. — St. Jerome

Prayer for Knowledge of Scripture

Lord, inspire us to read your Scriptures and to meditate upon them day and night. We beg you to give us real understanding of what we need, that we in turn may put its precepts into practice. Yet we know that understanding and good intentions are worthless, unless rooted in your graceful love. So we ask that the words of Scripture may also be not just signs on a page, but channels of grace into our hearts. Amen.[46]

— Attributed to Origen

PRAYERS FROM THE PSALMS

Psalm 23
Psalm of Comfort

The LORD is my shepherd,
   I shall not want;
He makes me lie down in green pastures.
He leads me beside still waters;
   he restores my soul.

He leads me in the paths of righteousness
  for his name's sake.

Even though I walk through the
      valley of the shadow of death,
  I fear no evil;
for thou art with me;
  thy rod and thy staff, they comfort me.

Thou preparest a table before me
  in the presence of my enemies;
thou anointest my head with oil,
  my cup overflows.
Surely goodness and mercy shall follow me.
  all the days of my life;
and I shall dwell in the house of the LORD
  forever.

Psalm 34:1-4
Psalm of Thanksgiving

I will bless the LORD at all times;
  his praise shall continually be in my mouth.
My soul makes its boast in the Lord;
  let the afflicted hear and be glad.
O magnify the LORD with me,
and let us exalt his name together!
I sought the LORD, and he answered me,
  and delivered me from all my fears.

Psalm 115:14
A Blessing

May the LORD give you increase,
  you and your children!

May you be blessed by the LORD,
who made heaven and earth!

Psalm 130
(De Profundis) *In Difficult Times*

Out of the depths I cry to thee,
O LORD!
LORD, hear my voice!
Let thy ears be attentive
to the voice of my supplications!

If thou, O LORD, shouldst mark iniquities,
LORD, who could stand?
But there is forgiveness with thee,
that thou mayest be feared.

I wait for the LORD, my soul waits,
and in his word I hope;
my soul waits for the LORD
more than watchmen for the morning,
more than watchmen for the morning.

O Israel, hope for the LORD!
For with the LORD there is steadfast love,
and with him is plenteous redemption.
And he will redeem Israel from all its iniquities.

Psalm 143:10
For Guidance

Teach me to do thy will,
for thou art my God!
Let thy good spirit lead me
on a level path!

Basics of the Catholic Faith

"Go therefore and make disciples of all nations, baptizing them in the name of the Father and of the Son and of the Holy Spirit, teaching them to observe all that I have commanded you; and lo, I am with you always, to the close of the age."

— MT. 28:18-20

The Seven Sacraments

Baptism
Confirmation
Holy Eucharist
Reconciliation or Penance
Anointing of the Sick
Holy Orders
Matrimony

The Ten Commandments

1. I, the Lord, am your God. You shall not have other gods besides me.

2. You shall not take the name of the Lord, your God, in vain.
3. Remember to keep holy the Sabbath day.
4. Honor your father and your mother.
5. You shall not kill.
6. You shall not commit adultery.
7. You shall not steal.
8. You shall not bear false witness against your neighbor.
9. You shall not covet your neighbor's wife.
10. You shall not covet your neighbor's goods.

(See Ex. 20:1-17 and Deut. 5:6-22.)

The Two Great Commandments

"You shall love the Lord your God with all your heart, and with all your soul, and with all your mind."
"You shall love your neighbor as yourself."

(When asked which commandment is the greatest, this was Jesus' answer. See Mt. 22:36-39.)

The Eight Beatitudes

1. Blessed are the poor in spirit, for theirs is the kingdom of heaven.
2. Blessed are those who mourn, for they shall be comforted.
3. Blessed are the meek, for they shall inherit the earth.
4. Blessed are those who hunger and thirst for righteousness, for they shall be satisfied.
5. Blessed are the merciful, for they shall obtain mercy.

6. Blessed are the pure in heart, for they shall see God.
7. Blessed are the peacemakers, for they shall be called sons of God.
8. Blessed are those who are persecuted for righteousness' sake, for theirs is the kingdom of heaven.

(See Mt. 5:3-10.)

The Corporal Works of Mercy

1. Feed the hungry.
2. Give drink to the thirsty.
3. Clothe the naked.
4. Visit the imprisoned.
5. Shelter the homeless.
6. Visit the sick.
7. Bury the dead.

The Spiritual Works of Mercy

1. Admonish the sinner.
2. Instruct the ignorant.
3. Counsel the doubtful.
4. Comfort the sorrowful.
5. Bear wrongs patiently.
6. Forgive all injuries.
7. Pray for the living and the dead.

Precepts of the Church

1. You shall attend Mass on Sundays and on holy days of obligation and rest from servile labor.
2. You shall confess your sins at least once a year.
3. You shall receive the sacrament of the Eucharist at least during the Easter season.
4. You shall observe the days of fasting and abstinence established by the Church.
5. You shall help to provide for the needs of the Church.

(These are meant to be the minimum Catholics should do.)

Gifts of the Holy Spirit

Wisdom
Understanding
Counsel
Fortitude

Knowledge
Piety
Fear of the Lord

Fruits of the Holy Spirit

Charity
Joy
Peace
Patience
Kindness
Goodness

Generosity
Gentleness
Faithfulness
Modesty
Self-control
Chastity

Capital Sins and the
Virtues They Oppose

Capital Sins	*Virtues Opposed*
Pride	Humility
Covetousness	Liberality
Lust	Chastity
Anger	Meekness
Gluttony	Temperance
Envy	Brotherly love
Sloth	Diligence

Cardinal Virtues

Prudence   Fortitude

Justice   Temperance

Theological Virtues

Faith   Hope   Charity

Notes

✛

[1] From *Manual of Prayers*, Rev. James D. Watkins, compiler. © 1996, 1998 by the American College of the Roman Catholic Church in the United States, published in the U.S. by Midwest Theological Forum (Chicago, IL) and Our Sunday Visitor Publishing (Huntington, IN).

[2] From *Manual of Prayers*.

[3] From *Your Prayer Book* by Rev. John A. O'Brien, Ph.D. © 1954 by John A. O'Brien, published by Our Sunday Visitor Publishing (Huntington, IN).

[4] From *A Book of Prayers*, copyright © 1982, by the International Committee on English in the Liturgy, Inc. (ICEL).

[5] From the Sacramentary, *Rite of Holy Week*.

[6] From *A Prayer Book for Young Catholics* by Father Robert Fox (Huntington, IN: Our Sunday Visitor Publishing, 1981).

[7] From *Your Prayer Book*.

[8] From *Embraced by Mary* by Rawley Myers (Huntington, IN: Our Sunday Visitor, 1997).

[9] From *Manual of Prayers*.

[10] From http://saints.catholic.org/saints/andrebessette.html copyright © Terry Metz.

[11] From *Manual of Prayers*.

[12] Adapted from www.catholic-forum.com.

[13] From *Manual of Prayers*.

[14] From *Manual of Prayers*.

[15] From *Manual of Prayers*.

[16] From *Manual of Prayers*.

[17] From *Manual of Prayers*.

[18] From the Bureau of Indian Missions.

[19] From National Shrine of St. Odilia, Onamia, MN 56359.

[20] From *Manual of Prayers.*

[21] From *Manual of Prayers.*

[22] Prayer from 1902.

[23] From *Manual of Prayers.*

[24] From *Manual of Prayers.*

[25] From *Manual of Prayers.*

[26] From *Handbook of Prayers,* Rev. James Socías, general editor. ©1992, 1995 by Rev. James Socías, Midwest Theological Forum, (Chicago, IL) and Our Sunday Visitor Publishing (Huntington, IN).

[27] From *A Book of Prayers.*

[28] From *A Book of Prayers.*

[29] From *Manual of Prayers.*

[30] From *Manual of Prayers.*

[31] From *A Prayer Book for Young Catholics.*

[32] From ICEL.

[33] From *Manual of Prayers.*

[34] Prayer from 1958.

[35] From ICEL.

[36] From *Pastoral Care of the Sick: Rites of Anointing and Viaticum,* ICEL.

[37] From *Order of Christian Funerals,* ICEL.

[38] From *Order of Christian Funerals.*

[39] From *Order of Christian Funerals.*

[40] From *Manual of Prayers.*

[41] From *Manual of Prayers.*

[42] From *Handbook of Prayers.*

[43] From *Manual of Prayers.*

[44] From *Manual of Prayers.*

[45] Prayer from the Diocese of Fort Wayne, August 15, 1958.

[46] From *Manual of Prayers.*

Index

✠